OXFORDSHIRE TRAVEL GUIDE 2024

Your ultimate county companion

Jan A. Ivey

THIS BOOK BELONGS TO:

TABLE OF
CONTENTS

INTRODUCTION TO OXFORDSHIRE

Oxfordshire, situated in the South East of England, boasts scenic landscapes, the globally acclaimed University of Oxford, and a storied history dating to the Saxon period. Charming towns, historic landmarks, and a lively cultural environment characterize the county. With a blend of natural allure and academic eminence, Oxfordshire presents a varied array of attractions catering to both visitors and residents. Whether you seek to delve into historical sites, partake in outdoor pursuits, or experience the dynamic city of Oxford, there's a wide range of offerings for all in Oxfordshire.

OVERVIEW OF OXFORDSHIRE

Oxfordshire is a captivating county located in the heart of England. Known for its rich history, stunning landscapes, and vibrant cultural scene, it offers a plethora of attractions and experiences for visitors.

At the center of Oxfordshire lies the city of Oxford, renowned for its prestigious University of Oxford, one of the oldest and most esteemed educational institutions in the world. The city is a captivating blend of historic architecture and modern energy, with picturesque streets, charming shops, and iconic landmarks.

Beyond Oxford, Oxfordshire boasts a diverse range of attractions. The county is home to magnificent palaces, such as Blenheim Palace, a UNESCO World Heritage Site and birthplace of Sir Winston Churchill. It also houses historic sites like Christ Church Cathedral, Bodleian Library, and Oxford Castle, each offering glimpses into the county's fascinating past.

Oxfordshire's natural beauty is equally captivating. The county is blessed with stunning countryside, charming villages, and tranquil waterways. Visitors can explore the enchanting Cotswolds, a designated Area of Outstanding Natural Beauty, or enjoy punting on the picturesque River Cherwell.

Cultural enthusiasts will find delight in Oxfordshire's world-class museums and galleries, including the Ashmolean Museum and Pitt Rivers Museum, which showcase art, history, and science. The county also hosts vibrant festivals, events, and a thriving arts and theater scene.

Oxfordshire's culinary offerings are diverse and enticing, with traditional pubs, fine dining establishments, and international cuisines to satisfy every palate. The county's shopping scene is equally impressive, with a mix of independent boutiques, high-end shops, and unique markets.

Whether you're a history buff, nature lover, culture enthusiast, or simply seeking a charming getaway,

Oxfordshire offers a captivating destination that combines centuries of heritage with modern allure.

HISTORY AND CULTURE

Oxfordshire has a rich history and vibrant culture that spans centuries.

History:

- Ancient Origins: The area that is now Oxfordshire has a history dating back to ancient times. Archaeological evidence suggests human presence in the region as early as the Mesolithic era, around 10,000 BC.

- Roman Occupation: The Romans arrived in Oxfordshire around the 1st century AD, establishing a settlement called "Oxonia" near the present-day city of Oxford. The Romans built roads and villas, leaving a lasting impact on the region.

- Anglo-Saxon and Viking Periods: Following the decline of the Roman

Empire, Oxfordshire came under the control of Anglo-Saxon kingdoms. The Vikings also made incursions into the region during the 9th and 10th centuries.

- University of Oxford: The University of Oxford, one of the oldest and most prestigious universities in the world, was founded in the 12th century. It played a significant role in shaping the intellectual and cultural landscape of Oxfordshire.

Cultural Heritage:

- Literary Connections: Oxfordshire has been a source of inspiration for renowned writers. J.R.R. Tolkien, author of "The Lord of the Rings," was a professor at the University of Oxford and drew inspiration from the county's landscapes. Lewis Carroll, author of

"Alice's Adventures in Wonderland," lived and worked in Oxfordshire, and C.S. Lewis, author of "The Chronicles of Narnia," was affiliated with the university.

- Arts and Theater: Oxfordshire has a thriving arts and theater scene. The county hosts the Oxfordshire Artweeks, a festival celebrating local artists, and the Oxford Playhouse, a renowned theater that showcases a diverse range of performances.

- Museums and Libraries: Oxfordshire is home to world-class museums and libraries. The Ashmolean Museum, founded in 1683, is the oldest public museum in the UK and houses extensive collections of art and archaeology. The Bodleian Library, part of the University of Oxford, is one of the largest and most prestigious libraries in the world, housing rare books and manuscripts.

- Festivals and Events: Oxfordshire hosts a variety of festivals and events throughout the year. The Oxford Literary Festival brings together renowned authors and literary enthusiasts, while the Cowley Road Carnival celebrates diversity and multiculturalism in the county.

Historic Landmarks:

- Oxford: The city of Oxford is a treasure trove of historic landmarks. Christ Church Cathedral, part of Christ Church College, is a magnificent example of Gothic and Romanesque architecture. The Bodleian Library, with its iconic Radcliffe Camera, is a symbol of Oxford's academic heritage. The Sheldonian Theatre, designed by Sir

Christopher Wren, is a notable venue for university ceremonies and events.

- Blenheim Palace: Located in Woodstock, Blenheim Palace is a UNESCO World Heritage Site and birthplace of Sir Winston Churchill. The grand palace, surrounded by beautiful gardens and parkland, is a masterpiece of English Baroque architecture.

- Oxford Castle: Oxford Castle, dating back to the Norman period, offers insights into the county's medieval history. Visitors can explore the castle's towers, crypts, and prison cells, and learn about its transformation into a cultural hub.

- Broughton Castle: Broughton Castle, a well-preserved medieval fortress located near Banbury, showcases the county's architectural heritage. It boasts a moat, impressive fortifications, and elegant interiors.

The history and culture of Oxfordshire are intertwined with its prestigious university, literary connections, historic landmarks, and vibrant arts scene. Visitors to Oxfordshire can immerse themselves in a rich tapestry of heritage, explore captivating museums, enjoy theatrical performances, and discover the enduring influence of this remarkable county.

PLANNING YOUR TRIP

Planning a trip to Oxfordshire can be an exciting endeavor. How to plan your trip to Oxfordshire:

1. *Determine the Duration: Decide how long you intend to stay in Oxfordshire. Consider the number of days you have available and how much time you want to allocate to exploring the county.*

2. *Research and Identify Attractions: Oxfordshire offers a wide range of attractions, from historic landmarks to natural*

beauty spots. Research and make a list of the places you want to visit, such as Oxford University, Blenheim Palace, Cotswolds villages, and museums. Prioritize based on your interests and the time available.

3. *Plan Accommodation: Look for accommodation options in Oxfordshire that suit your budget and preferences. Oxford city center is a popular choice, but you can also consider staying in charming towns or villages within the county. Book accommodations well in advance, especially during peak travel seasons.*

4. *Transportation: Determine how you will travel to and within Oxfordshire. If arriving by air, you can fly into nearby airports such as London Heathrow or Birmingham, and then take a train or hire a car to reach Oxfordshire. Public transportation, such as trains and buses, can be convenient for getting around the county, but renting a car offers more flexibility, especially for exploring rural areas.*

5. *Create an Itinerary: Develop a rough itinerary based on the attractions you wish to visit. Consider the opening hours of places you plan to see and plan your days accordingly. Allow*

some flexibility in your schedule to accommodate unexpected discoveries or additional activities.

6. *Check for Special Events: Oxfordshire hosts various events and festivals throughout the year. Check the local event calendars to see if any coincide with your travel dates. Attending a festival or special event can enhance your experience and provide unique insights into the local culture.*

7. *Pack Accordingly: Pack appropriate clothing and essentials based on the time of year and activities you plan to*

engage in. Comfortable walking shoes, weather-appropriate attire, and any specific gear for outdoor activities are recommended.

8. *Stay Informed: Stay updated on any travel advisories, entry requirements, or COVID-19 guidelines that may be in place during your visit. Check official websites and consult with relevant authorities for the most accurate and current information.*

9. *Explore Dining and Shopping: Oxfordshire offers a variety of dining options, from traditional pubs to fine dining*

*establishments. Research and
make a list of recommended
restaurants or local specialties
you'd like to try. Also, explore
the shopping scenes in Oxford
and other towns for unique
souvenirs, local products, or
antiques.*

*10.   Be Open to Discoveries:
While planning is essential, leave
room for spontaneous
explorations and unexpected
discoveries. Sometimes the most
memorable experiences are the
ones you stumble upon while
wandering the streets or
exploring the countryside.*

16

By following these steps, you can create a well-rounded plan for your trip to Oxfordshire, ensuring that you make the most of your time in this captivating county.

BEST TIME TO VISIT

The best time to visit Oxfordshire depends on your preferences and the activities you plan to engage in. Here's different seasons and factors to consider when deciding the best time to visit Oxfordshire:

Spring (March to May):

Spring is a delightful time to visit Oxfordshire. The weather begins to warm up, and the countryside bursts into vibrant colors as flowers bloom. The landscapes are lush and picturesque, making it an ideal time for outdoor activities such as walking, cycling, and exploring the countryside. Spring also coincides with the academic calendar, so you can

18

experience the lively atmosphere of the University of Oxford.

Summer (June to August):

Summer is a popular time to visit Oxfordshire, as the weather is generally warm and pleasant. The days are long, allowing for ample daylight to explore the attractions and enjoy outdoor activities. It is an excellent time to visit gardens, parks, and enjoy punting on the rivers. However, keep in mind that summer is the peak tourist season, and popular attractions can be crowded. It is advisable to book accommodations and attractions in advance.

Autumn (September to November):

Autumn in Oxfordshire is characterized by beautiful foliage as the leaves change color. The weather starts to cool down, and the crowds thin out compared to the summer months. It is a great time to visit if you prefer a quieter and more relaxed atmosphere. Autumn is also harvest season, and you can enjoy local produce, farmers' markets, and food festivals. The Cotswolds, with its charming villages, looks especially picturesque during this time of the year.

Winter (December to February):

Winter in Oxfordshire brings colder temperatures, but it can still be a charming time to visit. The city of Oxford, adorned with festive decorations, exudes a magical atmosphere during the holiday season. You can explore the museums, libraries, and indoor attractions, making it an ideal time for history and culture enthusiasts. Winter also offers opportunities for cozying up in traditional pubs and enjoying seasonal events and performances.

Factors to Consider:

1. *Weather: Consider your tolerance for different weather conditions. Summers are generally warm, while winters can be cold and wet. Choose a season that aligns with your preferred weather conditions.*

2. *Crowds: If you prefer a quieter experience with fewer tourists, consider visiting during the shoulder seasons (spring and*

autumn) when the crowds are thinner compared to summer.

3. *Events and Festivals: Check the event calendars for festivals, cultural events, or special exhibitions happening in Oxfordshire. Attending these events can enhance your visit and provide unique experiences.*

4. *University Calendar: Keep in mind that the academic calendar of the University of Oxford can influence the atmosphere in the city. If you want to experience the vibrant student life, visit during term time. However, if you prefer a quieter visit,*

*consider avoiding the peak
academic periods.*

5. *Budget: Prices for
   accommodations and attractions
   may vary depending on the
   season. Consider the cost
   implications when planning your
   trip.*

The best time to visit Oxfordshire will
depend on your personal preferences,
the activities you plan to engage in,
and the atmosphere you desire. Each
season offers its own unique charm
and opportunities to explore the
history, culture, and natural beauty of
this captivating county.

GETTING TO OXFORDSHIRE

Getting to Oxfordshire is relatively easy due to its central location within the United Kingdom. Different transportation options for reaching Oxfordshire:

By Air:

1. London Heathrow Airport: Located approximately 50 miles east of Oxfordshire, Heathrow is the busiest airport in the UK. From Heathrow, you can reach Oxfordshire by various means, including:

   - Train: Take the Heathrow Express to London Paddington station, then transfer to a train to Oxford or other destinations within Oxfordshire.

  - Bus: National Express and other bus companies operate services from Heathrow to Oxford and other towns in Oxfordshire.

  - Taxi or Private Transfer: Taxis and private transfer services are available for direct transportation to any destination in Oxfordshire.

2. Birmingham Airport: Situated about 65 miles north of Oxfordshire, Birmingham Airport is another option for reaching the county. From the airport, you can:

  - Take a direct train to Oxford or other towns in Oxfordshire.

  - Hire a taxi or use private transfer services to reach your destination.

By Train:

Oxfordshire is well-connected to the national rail network, making train travel a convenient option. The main railway station is Oxford station, located in the city of Oxford. Direct trains operate from various major cities in the UK, including London, Birmingham, and Manchester. There are also frequent connections to other towns in Oxfordshire, such as Banbury, Didcot, and Bicester. Train services are provided by operators like Great Western Railway (GWR) and Chiltern Railways.

By Car:

Oxfordshire is easily accessible by road, and driving is a popular option for reaching the county. Major roads that connect to Oxfordshire include:

- M40: Connects Oxfordshire to London and the southeast of England.

- A34: Links Oxfordshire to major cities like Birmingham and Southampton.

- A40: Connects Oxfordshire to London and other towns in the Thames Valley.

Car rental services are available at major airports and in Oxford city. However, keep in mind that driving in Oxford city center can be challenging due to limited parking and traffic restrictions. It is advisable to use park-and-ride facilities or public transportation when exploring the city.

By Bus:

27

National Express and other bus companies operate services to Oxford and other towns in Oxfordshire from various locations across the UK. The bus station in Oxford is conveniently located near the city center. Bus services offer an affordable option for travel to Oxfordshire, but travel times may be longer compared to trains.

Local Transportation:

Once in Oxfordshire, there are several options for getting around:

- Public Transportation: Oxfordshire has a well-developed public transportation network, including buses and trains, which can be used to explore different parts of the county.

- Car Rental: Renting a car provides flexibility and convenience for exploring Oxfordshire, particularly rural areas and villages.

- Cycling: Oxfordshire is a cyclist-friendly county, with numerous cycling routes and dedicated paths. Bike rentals are available in Oxford.

- Walking: Oxfordshire offers beautiful countryside and scenic trails, making it an ideal destination for walking enthusiasts.

It's important to note that transportation options and schedules may vary, so it's advisable to check for the latest information and plan your journey accordingly.

TRANSPORTATION WITHIN OXFORDSHIRE

Oxfordshire offers a variety of transportation options for getting around the county.

1. Public Transportation:

   - Buses: Oxford Bus Company and Stagecoach are the main bus operators in Oxfordshire. They provide extensive bus services within the county, connecting major towns, villages, and attractions. Oxford's bus network is particularly comprehensive, with frequent services covering the city and surrounding areas.

   - Trains: Oxfordshire has a well-connected rail network, with regular train services operated by Great Western Railway (GWR) and Chiltern

Railways. Trains are a convenient option for traveling between different towns within Oxfordshire and also for reaching Oxfordshire from other parts of the UK.

- Park-and-Ride: Oxford operates park-and-ride services at various locations on the outskirts of the city. These services allow visitors to park their cars at designated parking lots and use dedicated bus services to travel into the city center, avoiding parking congestion.

2. Taxis and Private Hire:

- Taxis: Taxis can be found in most towns and cities in Oxfordshire, offering on-demand transportation. You can hail a taxi from designated taxi ranks or book one in advance.

- Private Hire: Private hire services, such as Uber and local minicab companies, operate in Oxfordshire. These services require pre-booking, and fares are usually determined in advance.

3. Cycling:

- Oxfordshire is a cyclist-friendly county, with numerous cycling paths, lanes, and trails. Oxford, in particular, has an extensive network of cycle routes. You can rent bicycles from various providers in Oxford and some other towns, allowing you to explore the county at your own pace.

4. Car Rental:

- Renting a car is a convenient option for exploring Oxfordshire, especially if you plan to visit rural areas, villages, or attractions outside the main towns. Car rental companies operate in Oxford and other major towns, providing a range of vehicle options.

5. Walking:

   - Oxfordshire offers picturesque countryside and scenic walking trails, making it an ideal destination for walkers. You can explore footpaths, bridleways, and national trails, such as the Thames Path or the Ridgeway.

6. Other Options:

   - Punting: In Oxford, you can experience punting, a traditional mode of transport on the rivers. Punting involves propelling a flat-bottomed boat with a long pole, and it's a popular activity along the River Cherwell and the River Thames.

   - Sightseeing Tours: Various companies offer guided sightseeing tours in Oxford and other parts of Oxfordshire. These tours provide transportation along with insightful commentary, allowing you to explore the highlights of the county.

It's worth noting that transportation options and schedules may vary depending on the specific location and time of day. It's advisable to check for the latest information, including bus and train timetables, and plan your journeys accordingly. Additionally, consider using navigation apps or consulting local tourist information centers for up-to-date transportation details.

35

ACCOMMODATION OPTIONS

In Oxfordshire, you'll find a wide range of accommodations to suit every preference and budget. From luxury hotels and charming bed and breakfasts to cozy countryside inns and self-catering cottages, there are plenty of options to choose from. If you prefer the convenience of staying in the city, you can find modern hotels with all the amenities you need for a comfortable stay. For a more tranquil experience, you can opt for a stay in one of the county's many idyllic rural retreats, offering a peaceful escape surrounded by stunning landscapes. Additionally, there are options for those looking for a more budget-friendly stay, including hostels and guesthouses. Whether you're visiting for business or pleasure, you'll find the perfect place to rest your head in Oxfordshire.

HOTELS AND INNS IN OXFORDSHIRE

Oxfordshire offers a range of hotels and inns to cater to different preferences and budgets.

BUDGET FRIENDLY OPTIONS

1. *The Feathers, Woodstock: Located in the charming town of Woodstock, near Blenheim Palace, this historic hotel combines traditional features with modern comforts. It offers comfortable rooms, a restaurant serving British cuisine, and a cozy bar. The Feathers is a*

popular choice for visitors exploring the Cotswolds.

2. *The Bear Hotel, Woodstock: A historic coaching inn dating back to the 13th century, situated in the heart of Woodstock. It offers comfortable rooms, a restaurant serving British classics, and a traditional pub atmosphere. The Bear Hotel is a cozy and characterful option.*

3. *The Lamb Inn, Burford: A traditional inn nestled in the picturesque town of Burford. It features cozy rooms with period features, a restaurant serving British dishes, and a welcoming bar. The Lamb Inn is well-placed*

for exploring the Cotswolds region.

4. *The Kingham Plough, Kingham: Located in the charming village of Kingham, this inn offers comfortable rooms, a restaurant showcasing locally sourced ingredients, and a relaxed atmosphere. The Kingham Plough is a popular choice for food lovers exploring the Cotswolds.*

5. *The Crown Inn, Chipping Norton: Situated in the market town of Chipping Norton, this historic inn offers comfortable rooms, a traditional pub ambiance, and a restaurant serving seasonal*

British cuisine. The Crown Inn is well-positioned for exploring the Cotswolds and nearby attractions.

6. *The Bear and Ragged Staff, Oxfordshire: Located in the village of Cumnor, just outside Oxford, this 13th-century coaching inn offers cozy rooms and a traditional English pub atmosphere. The Bear and Ragged Staff is known for its hearty food and picturesque surroundings, making it a charming countryside retreat.*

7. *The Chequers Inn, Cassington: Situated in the village of Cassington, close to Oxford, this traditional inn offers comfortable rooms and a cozy pub atmosphere. The Chequers Inn serves classic pub food and is known for its friendly service and relaxed ambiance.*

8. *The Crown and Thistle, Abingdon: Situated in the town of Abingdon-on-Thames, this historic coaching inn offers comfortable rooms and a traditional pub setting. The Crown and Thistle is known for its characterful interior, friendly service, and proximity to Abingdon's attractions and the River Thames.*

9. *The George Hotel, Wallingford: A 16th-century coaching inn located in the market town of Wallingford. The George Hotel offers comfortable rooms, a restaurant serving seasonal dishes, and a cozy bar. It's a great base for exploring Wallingford's history and the nearby Chiltern Hills.*

MID RANGE OPTIONS

1. *The Head of the River, Oxford: Situated on the banks of the River Thames, this historic inn provides comfortable rooms with river views. The Head of the River features a pub and restaurant serving classic British dishes, and its location offers easy access to the city center and popular landmarks like Christ Church College.*

2. *The Lambert Arms, Watlington: Situated in the Oxfordshire countryside, this traditional*

coaching inn provides comfortable accommodations and a warm, welcoming atmosphere. The Lambert Arms features a restaurant serving British and international cuisine, and it's a great base for exploring the Chiltern Hills and nearby attractions.

3. *The Oxford Belfry, Thame: A modern hotel located in the village of Milton Common, near Thame. The Oxford Belfry offers spacious rooms, a leisure club with a swimming pool and gym, and a restaurant serving contemporary cuisine. It's a convenient choice for both business and leisure travelers.*

4. *The Fleece at Witney, Witney:*
   Located in the market town of
   Witney, this historic inn features
   stylish rooms and a vibrant pub
   and restaurant. The Fleece is
   known for its modern British
   cuisine, extensive drink
   selection, and live music events.

LUXURIOUS OPTIONS

1. *The Randolph Hotel, Oxford: A*
   renowned luxury hotel located in
   the heart of Oxford. It offers
   elegant rooms, fine dining at the
   Acanthus Restaurant, and a
   traditional afternoon tea
   experience. The hotel's historic
   charm and central location make
   it a popular choice for visitors.

2. *Belmond Le Manoir aux Quat'Saisons, Great Milton: Situated in a picturesque village near Oxford, this luxury hotel and restaurant is a destination in itself. It features exquisite rooms, a two-Michelin-starred restaurant led by chef Raymond Blanc, beautiful gardens, and a cooking school.*

3. *The Crazy Bear Hotel, Stadhampton: A unique and lavish hotel known for its flamboyant décor and luxurious amenities. It offers individually designed rooms, a Thai restaurant, cocktail bars, and an English pub. The Crazy Bear*

provides a memorable and extravagant experience.

4. *The Old Parsonage Hotel, Oxford: A boutique hotel located in a historic building in Oxford. It offers stylish rooms, a restaurant serving modern British cuisine, and a cozy bar. The hotel's location near the city center makes it convenient for exploring Oxford's attractions.*

5. *The Old Bank Hotel, Oxford: Another boutique hotel situated in the heart of Oxford, overlooking the famous Radcliffe Camera. It features elegant rooms, a rooftop terrace, a contemporary restaurant, and a*

lively bar. The Old Bank Hotel offers a sophisticated and central base for exploring the city.

6. *Macdonald Randolph Hotel, Oxford: A grand Victorian hotel located in the city center of Oxford, close to attractions such as the Ashmolean Museum and Oxford University. The Macdonald Randolph Hotel offers spacious rooms, a spa and wellness center, and a popular Morse Bar, named after the famous detective created by Oxford author Colin Dexter.*

7. *Malmaison Oxford: Housed in a converted Victorian prison, this stylish boutique hotel offers contemporary rooms with unique*

features like iron doors and original brickwork. Malmaison Oxford is located near Oxford Castle and is known for its trendy atmosphere and brasserie-style dining.

These hotels and inns provide a diverse range of options for visitors to Oxfordshire, whether you're seeking luxury, historic charm, countryside ambiance, or convenient city center locations. Each establishment offers its own unique atmosphere and amenities, ensuring there's something to suit every traveler's preferences.

BED AND BREAKFAST ESTABLISHMENTS IN OXFORDSHIRE

Oxfordshire is home to numerous charming bed and breakfast establishments that offer comfortable accommodations and a more personal touch. These B&Bs often provide a warm and homely atmosphere, making them a popular choice among travelers seeking a cozy and intimate experience.

LUXURIOUS OPTIONS

1. *Cotswold House, Oxford:*
   Situated in the historic village of Woodstock, near Blenheim Palace, Cotswold House is a boutique bed and breakfast offering individually designed rooms with stylish decor. The B&B features a garden, a guest lounge, and a delicious breakfast made with locally sourced ingredients.

2. *The Oxford Townhouse, Oxford:*
   Located in the heart of Oxford, The Oxford Townhouse offers contemporary and comfortable rooms in a Victorian building. The B&B provides a complimentary breakfast and is within walking distance of Oxford's attractions, including

the Ashmolean Museum and the University of Oxford.

3. *The Dial House, Oxford: Set in a Georgian townhouse in the Jericho neighborhood of Oxford, The Dial House offers elegant and individually decorated rooms with modern amenities. Guests can enjoy a cooked breakfast each morning, and the B&B is conveniently located near Oxford's city center and attractions.*

4. *The Osney Arms Guest House, Oxford: Situated in the lively Jericho neighborhood of Oxford, The Osney Arms Guest House offers comfortable and affordable*

rooms. The B&B includes a complimentary breakfast and is conveniently situated near restaurants, cafes, and the University of Oxford.

MIDRANGE OPTIONS

5. *The Old Post Office, Wallingford: Situated in the market town of Wallingford, The Old Post Office is a cozy B&B housed in a historic building. The B&B features comfortable rooms, a garden, and a delicious breakfast served in a charming dining area. It's a great choice for exploring Wallingford and the surrounding area.*

6. *The Highwayman Hotel, Kidlington: Located just outside Oxford, The Highwayman Hotel is a traditional pub with comfortable rooms available as a bed and breakfast option. The B&B offers a warm and friendly atmosphere, an on-site pub serving hearty meals, and easy access to Oxford and the Cotswolds.*

7. *The Tally Ho Hotel, Bicester: Situated in the village of Arncott, near Bicester, The Tally Ho Hotel is a family-run bed and breakfast offering comfortable accommodations and a traditional pub atmosphere. The B&B features cozy rooms, a restaurant serving homemade*

dishes, and is conveniently located for exploring Bicester Village and the surrounding areas.

8. The Dashwood, Kirtlington: Nestled in a picturesque village near Oxford, The Dashwood is a family-run B&B housed in a traditional stone cottage. It offers comfortable rooms with country-style décor and a delicious breakfast. The B&B is surrounded by beautiful countryside and is a great choice for those seeking a peaceful retreat.

9. The Old Farmhouse, Wallingford: Located in the village of

*Crowmarsh Gifford, near
Wallingford, The Old Farmhouse
is a charming B&B housed in a
15th-century thatched cottage. It
features cozy rooms with
exposed beams and a hearty
breakfast made with locally
sourced produce. The B&B is
ideally situated for exploring
Wallingford and nearby walking
trails.*

10.   *The Old Swan & Minster
Mill, Minster Lovell: Situated in
the picturesque village of Minster
Lovell, this B&B offers a
combination of traditional inn
rooms and self-contained
cottage-style rooms. Set in a
historic building, The Old Swan &
Minster Mill features a
restaurant, a bar, and beautiful*

gardens along the River Windrush.

11.   The Cleve, Swinbrook: Located in the idyllic village of Swinbrook, near Burford, The Cleve is a charming B&B housed in a historic building. It offers comfortable rooms with elegant décor and serves a delicious breakfast. Guests can enjoy the peaceful countryside surroundings and explore the nearby Cotswold villages.

12.   The Holt Hotel, Steeple Aston: Situated near Bicester, The Holt Hotel is a traditional B&B housed in a 15th-century coaching inn. It offers comfortable rooms, a restaurant serving classic British dishes, and a cozy bar. The B&B is conveniently located for exploring Bicester Village and Oxfordshire's attractions.

13.   *The Bell, Charlbury: Located in the Cotswold town of Charlbury, The Bell is a charming B&B housed in a 17th-century building. It offers comfortable rooms with period features and a restaurant serving seasonal dishes. The B&B is surrounded by scenic countryside and is a great base for exploring the Cotswolds.*

BUDGET FRIENDLY OPTIONS

14.   Green Gables Guest House, Oxford: Located in the Headington area of Oxford, Green Gables Guest House provides comfortable rooms in a Victorian house. The B&B offers a friendly and welcoming environment, a delicious breakfast, and easy access to Oxford's hospitals, universities, and city center.

15.   Ashbrook Lets, Abingdon: Situated in the town of Abingdon-on-Thames, Ashbrook Lets offers self-contained apartments and rooms with private entrances. The B&B provides a comfortable and flexible stay, with each unit

*featuring a kitchenette and
modern amenities.*

16.   *The Old Court Hotel,
Witney: Located in the market
town of Witney, The Old Court
Hotel is a charming B&B set in a
historic building. The B&B offers
cozy rooms, a garden, and a
restaurant serving traditional
British cuisine. It's a great base
for exploring Witney and the
Cotswolds.*

17.   *The Buttery, Oxford:
Located in the heart of Oxford,
The Buttery is a historic building
converted into a charming B&B.
It offers cozy rooms with modern
amenities. Guests can enjoy a
continental breakfast and explore*

the city's attractions, such as the Bodleian Library and Oxford Castle.

18.   The Plough Inn, Kelmscott: Situated in the picturesque village of Kelmscott, The Plough Inn is a cozy B&B with a traditional pub atmosphere. It provides comfortable rooms and serves hearty meals using locally sourced ingredients. Guests can also explore the nearby Kelmscott Manor, the former home of William Morris.

19.   The Crown Inn, Benson: located in the picturesque village of Benson near Wallingford, offers traditional B&B accommodation with comfortable rooms and a welcoming ambiance. Additionally, guests can enjoy the on-site restaurant serving British cuisine and a cozy bar. Its location makes it an excellent choice for those looking to explore the stunning Thames Valley area.

20.	The Old Post Office, Shipton-under-Wychwood: situated in a historic 17th-century building in the village of Shipton-under-Wychwood, provides comfortable accommodation, a charming garden, and a delectable breakfast for guests to enjoy. Surrounded by scenic countryside, this B&B serves as an ideal starting point for exploring the Cotswolds.

These represent selection of the bed and breakfast accommodations offered in Oxfordshire. Each B&B boasts a distinctive ambiance and level of service, guaranteeing an enjoyable experience for guests visiting the region.

UNIVERSITY ACCOMODATIONS IN OXFORDSHIRE

Oxfordshire is home to the prestigious University of Oxford, and the city of Oxford itself offers a range of university accommodations. These accommodations are primarily aimed at students, visiting scholars, and conference attendees. While availability may vary depending on the time of year and specific events, here are some types of university accommodations in Oxfordshire:

1. *College Rooms: Many of the colleges at the University of Oxford offer rooms for short-term stays during vacation periods. These rooms are often located within historic college buildings and provide a unique experience of staying in an academic and cultural setting. Some colleges that offer accommodations include Christ Church, Magdalen College, Pembroke College, and St Edmund Hall, among others.*

2. *University Halls of Residence: The University of Oxford also operates various halls of*

residence that provide accommodation for students during term time. These halls may offer rooms on a short-term basis during vacation periods. Examples of university halls of residence include Wolfson College, St Anne's College, and Lady Margaret Hall.

3. *Summer Conferences and Events: During the summer months, many colleges and universities in Oxfordshire open their accommodations to external visitors attending conferences, workshops, or summer schools. This allows individuals and groups to stay in university facilities while participating in academic or cultural events. The*

University of Oxford Conference Oxford program provides information about the availability of such accommodations.

4. *Graduate Accommodations: Some colleges at the University of Oxford have dedicated accommodations for graduate students, including both long-term and short-term stays. These accommodations are designed to meet the specific needs of postgraduate students and may be available for short-term bookings during vacation periods.*

It's important to note that availability, pricing, and booking procedures for university accommodations in Oxfordshire can vary. It's advisable to check with individual colleges or the University of Oxford's accommodation office for up-to-date information, availability, and booking procedures. Additionally, there are also private accommodation options available in and around Oxford, which may be suitable for short-term stays and visiting scholars.

SELF CATERING ACCOMODATION OPTIONS

Oxfordshire offers a variety of self-catering accommodations, ranging from cottages and apartments to holiday homes and lodges. Website such as Airbnb, HomeAway and booking.com offer a range of options at different price rates. These options provide visitors with the flexibility and convenience of preparing their meals while enjoying the comforts of a private space. Here are some self-catering accommodations in Oxfordshire:

1. *Cotswold Holiday Cottages, Oxfordshire: This agency offers a selection of self-catering cottages throughout Oxfordshire, including in popular areas like the Cotswolds and the Thames Valley. These cottages range from traditional stone properties to modern apartments, providing guests with a range of options to choose from.*

2. The Old Dairy, Oxford: Situated in the village of Noke, near Oxford, The Old Dairy offers self-catering accommodation in a converted barn. The property features well-appointed cottages with fully equipped kitchens, comfortable living areas, and access to a garden. It's a peaceful retreat within easy reach of Oxford's attractions.

3. The Stables, Henley-on-Thames: Located near the town of Henley-on-Thames, The Stables is a self-catering cottage set within a tranquil countryside estate. The cottage offers modern amenities, a fully equipped kitchen, and a private garden. Guests can enjoy

the beautiful surroundings and explore the nearby Chiltern Hills.

4. The Keepers' Cottage, Woodstock: Situated on the Blenheim Palace estate in Woodstock, The Keepers' Cottage is a self-catering property in a secluded location. The cottage features a well-equipped kitchen, spacious living areas, and access to the palace's extensive grounds. It's a unique opportunity to stay in a historic setting.

5. Swereview Cottage, Banbury: Located in the village of Swalcliffe, near Banbury, Swereview Cottage is a charming self-catering accommodation surrounded by picturesque countryside. The cottage offers a fully equipped kitchen, comfortable bedrooms, and a garden. It's a great base for exploring the Cotswolds and nearby attractions.

6. *The Old Bakehouse, Burford: Situated in the historic market town of Burford, The Old Bakehouse is a self-catering cottage with character. The cottage features a well-equipped kitchen, cozy living spaces, and a courtyard garden. It's conveniently located for exploring the Cotswolds and enjoying the amenities of Burford.*

7. *The Coach House, Witney:
   Located in the town of Witney,
   The Coach House is a self-
   catering property set within a
   private courtyard. The house
   offers a fully equipped kitchen,
   comfortable bedrooms, and a
   patio area. It's a convenient base
   for exploring both Oxfordshire
   and the Cotswolds.*

8. *The Lodge, Bicester: Situated in
   the village of Ambrosden, near
   Bicester, The Lodge is a self-
   catering property set within a
   peaceful garden. The lodge
   features a well-equipped kitchen,
   comfortable bedrooms, and a
   private patio. It's a relaxing
   retreat within easy reach of*

Bicester Village and Oxfordshire's attractions.

9. *The Granary, Chipping Norton: Located near the town of Chipping Norton, The Granary is a self-catering cottage set within a picturesque farm estate. The cottage offers modern amenities, a fully equipped kitchen, and access to a communal garden. Guests can enjoy the tranquility of the countryside and explore the Cotswolds.*

10. *The Studio, Wallingford: Situated in the town of Wallingford, The Studio is a self-contained apartment offering comfortable and modern*

*accommodation. The apartment
features a well-equipped
kitchenette, a comfortable living
area, and access to a garden. It's
a convenient choice for exploring
Wallingford and the surrounding
area.*

These self-catering accommodations in
Oxfordshire offer guests the flexibility
to explore the region at their leisure,
all while enjoying the conveniences of
a private dwelling. Whether seeking a
rural cottage or a downtown
apartment, a variety of options are
available to accommodate different
preferences and group sizes.

TRAVEL TIPS AND ESSENTIAL INFORMATION

1. *Best Time to Visit: Oxfordshire has a mild climate, with summers being the peak tourist season. For a more relaxed visit and better deals, consider visiting during the spring (March to May) or autumn (September to November) when the weather is pleasant and the crowds are fewer.*

2. *Transportation: Oxford has a well-developed public transportation system, including an extensive bus network operated by companies such as the Oxford Bus Company and Stagecoach. Consider purchasing*

a contactless payment card or day pass for convenience. Additionally, trains provide connections to Oxford from major cities in the UK.

3. *Parking: While driving to Oxford, it's important to note that parking can be limited and expensive in the city center. It is recommended to utilize one of the Park and Ride locations on the outskirts of the city and take the bus into the city for a more convenient parking experience.*

4. *Walking and cycling are popular modes of transportation in Oxford due to its compact size and the proximity of attractions.*

Exploring on foot allows for a deeper appreciation of the city's historic charm, while cycling is also a common activity with bicycle rentals available at various locations.

5. *When visiting the University of Oxford colleges and other attractions, it is advised to dress modestly and refrain from wearing revealing or beach attire. Certain locations may have specific dress code policies in place for entry.*

6. *Although credit and debit cards are widely accepted in Oxfordshire, it is advisable to carry some cash for smaller*

purchases, market stalls, or establishments that may not accept card payments. ATMs are easily accessible in Oxford city center and surrounding towns.

7. Safety: Oxfordshire is generally a safe destination, but it's always advisable to take common precautions. Keep an eye on your belongings, especially in crowded areas, and be cautious of your surroundings, particularly at night.

8. Visitor Information Centers: Oxford has a Visitor Information Center located on Broad Street, where you can obtain maps, brochures, and advice from

helpful staff. They can provide information about attractions, events, and any current promotions.

9. *Opening Hours: Keep in mind that opening hours may vary for attractions, especially during weekends and public holidays. It's a good idea to check the websites or contact the specific attractions you plan to visit for up-to-date information on opening times.*

10. *Wi-Fi and Connectivity: Many cafes, restaurants, and public spaces in Oxford offer free Wi-Fi access. Additionally, major mobile network operators*

*provide good coverage
throughout the region.*

These tips and essential information should help you navigate and enjoy your visit to Oxfordshire. Remember to plan ahead, check specific attraction websites for any updates, and make the most of the rich history, cultural attractions, and natural beauty the region has to offer!

EXPLORING OXFORD

Exploring Oxford is a delightful experience, offering a mix of historical landmarks, cultural attractions, and picturesque scenery. Begin your day with a visit to the University of Oxford, renowned for its stunning architecture and rich academic history. Take a leisurely stroll through the college courtyards and marvel at the Bodleian Library, the Radcliffe Camera, and the Sheldonian Theatre.

Continue your exploration with a walk along the tranquil banks of the River Thames or the River Cherwell, where you can enjoy punting or simply relax by the water. Don't miss the opportunity to visit the Ashmolean Museum, home to a diverse collection of art and artifacts spanning centuries of history.

For a taste of Oxford's literary heritage, pay a visit to the Eagle and Child pub, a historic meeting place for the famous literary group known as the Inklings, which included authors like J.R.R. Tolkien and C.S. Lewis.

Finally, cap off your day with a visit to the iconic Christ Church College, which served as inspiration for the Harry Potter films. Its grand dining hall and beautiful meadow are must-see attractions.

With its blend of academic allure, natural beauty, and cultural significance, exploring Oxford promises a captivating and enriching experience for visitors.

How to make the most of your visit:

1. *Historic Colleges: Start your exploration by visiting the University of Oxford's historic colleges. Be sure to visit iconic colleges such as Christ Church, Magdalen College, and New College, each with its own unique architectural features and stunning gardens.*

2. *Bodleian Library: Discover the Bodleian Library, one of the oldest libraries in Europe. Take a guided tour to explore its impressive collection, including*

historic manuscripts and the magnificent Radcliffe Camera, an iconic Oxford landmark.

3. *Radcliffe Square: Stroll through Radcliffe Square, surrounded by architectural gems like the Radcliffe Camera, the Sheldonian Theatre, and the University Church of St Mary the Virgin. Climb the tower of St Mary's Church for panoramic views of Oxford.*

4. *Covered Market: Visit the historic Covered Market, a vibrant hub of local traders offering a variety of goods, from fresh produce to unique gifts and delicious food. Don't miss trying the famous*

Oxfordshire sausage or indulging in a traditional afternoon tea.

5. *Ashmolean Museum: Explore the Ashmolean Museum, the oldest public museum in the UK. It houses a diverse collection of art and artifacts, spanning centuries and civilizations. Marvel at ancient Egyptian mummies, Renaissance masterpieces, and contemporary artworks.*

6. *River Thames and Punting: Take a leisurely walk along the banks of the River Thames (known as the Isis in Oxford). For a quintessentially Oxford experience, go punting on the river, where you can glide along*

while admiring the beautiful scenery and passing by picturesque college boathouses.

7. Oxford Botanic Garden: Escape the bustling city and wander through the peaceful Oxford Botanic Garden. Discover an array of plant species from around the world, explore themed gardens, and relax in the tranquil surroundings.

8. Museums and Galleries: Oxford is home to several other museums and galleries worth exploring, such as the Museum of Natural History, Pitt Rivers Museum, and Modern Art Oxford. These institutions offer fascinating

*exhibits and displays that cater
to various interests.*

9. *Harry Potter Connections: For
   fans of the Harry Potter series,
   Oxford offers connections to the
   movies. Visit locations like the
   Bodleian Library's Divinity
   School, which served as the
   Hogwarts Infirmary, or Christ
   Church's Great Hall, which
   inspired the iconic Hogwarts
   dining hall.*

10. *Local Events and Festivals:
    Keep an eye out for local events
    and festivals happening in Oxford
    during your visit. From literary
    festivals to music events and
    Christmas markets, there's often*

*something exciting taking place
that adds to the vibrant
atmosphere of the city.*

*11.   Museum of Natural History:
Located in a stunning Victorian
building, the Museum of Natural
History showcases a vast array
of natural specimens, including
dinosaur skeletons, fossils,
minerals, and taxidermy exhibits.
Don't miss the famous Dodo
specimen and the Oxfordshire
dinosaurs.*

*12.   Pitt Rivers Museum:
Connected to the Museum of
Natural History, the Pitt Rivers
Museum houses an extensive
collection of anthropological and
archaeological artifacts from*

around the world. Its unique display style, organized by themes rather than geographical regions, offers a fascinating glimpse into different cultures.

13.   *Oxford Castle and Prison: Go on a guided tour of the Oxford Castle and Prison to uncover the city's dark history. Explore the atmospheric underground crypt, climb the Saxon St. George's Tower for panoramic views, and learn about the castle's role in England's history.*

14.   *Christ Church Cathedral: Visit the magnificent Christ Church Cathedral, the spiritual*

*heart of the University of Oxford.
Admire the stunning
architecture, intricate stained
glass windows, and the tranquil
cloisters. You can also climb the
cathedral tower for breathtaking
views of Oxford's skyline.*

15.   *Oxford Covered Market:
Immerse yourself in the bustling
atmosphere of the Oxford
Covered Market. Wander through
its narrow lanes lined with a
variety of independent shops,
boutiques, food stalls, and
traditional pubs. Sample local
treats like Oxfordshire cheeses,
artisan chocolates, and freshly
baked goods.*

16.   *Oxford University Museum of the History of Science: Delve into the world of scientific discoveries at the Museum of the History of Science. Learn about the instruments used by famous scientists like Albert Einstein and explore exhibits on astronomy, chemistry, and early medical practices.*

17.   *Botley Road and Jericho: Wander beyond the city center to explore the vibrant neighborhoods of Botley Road and Jericho. Here, you'll find a mix of independent shops, trendy cafes, and cozy pubs. Enjoy a leisurely stroll along the Oxford Canal and discover the area's unique charm.*

18.   *Blenheim Palace: Just outside Oxford, you'll find Blenheim Palace, a UNESCO World Heritage Site and the birthplace of Sir Winston Churchill. Explore the opulent palace interiors, stroll through the magnificent gardens, and enjoy the peaceful parkland.*

19.   *Oxfordshire Countryside: Take a break from the city and venture into the picturesque Oxfordshire countryside. Visit charming villages like Woodstock, Burford, and Bampton (known as the setting for the fictional village of Downton in the TV series "Downton Abbey"). Enjoy scenic*

walks, visit historic churches, and soak in the idyllic rural landscapes.

20. Literary Connections: Oxford has strong literary ties, being the home of renowned authors like J.R.R. Tolkien, C.S. Lewis, and Lewis Carroll. Explore places that inspired their works, such as the Eagle and Child pub (where the Inklings literary group met), the Alice's Shop (inspiration for "Alice in Wonderland"), and the Tolkien Trail at the University Parks.

Remember to wear comfortable shoes, as Oxford is best explored on foot, and allow yourself time to simply wander and soak in the unique atmosphere of this historic city. Enjoy exploring Oxford's rich heritage, academic excellence, and cultural treasures!

OXFORD CITY CENTER

Oxford City Center is a vibrant and historic area that forms the heart of the city. It is known for its prestigious university, stunning architecture, charming streets, and a wealth of cultural and historical attractions. Here's a breakdown of what you can expect to find in Oxford City Center:

1. *Radcliffe Square: This iconic square is home to architectural gems such as the Radcliffe Camera, a circular library, and*

the University Church of St Mary
the Virgin. The square is
surrounded by historic buildings
and offers a picturesque setting
for a leisurely stroll.

2. High Street: The bustling High
   Street, also known as the "The
   High," runs through the center of
   Oxford. It is lined with an array
   of shops, boutiques, cafes, and
   restaurants. Take a leisurely
   walk along this vibrant street and
   soak in the lively atmosphere.

3. Carfax Tower: Located at the
   junction of High Street, Queen
   Street, St Aldate's, and
   Cornmarket Street, Carfax Tower
   provides panoramic views of the

city center. Climb the tower for stunning vistas of Oxford's spires, rooftops, and surrounding landscapes.

4. *Covered Market: The historic Covered Market is a must-visit destination in the city center. It houses a wide range of independent shops, food stalls, cafes, and traditional pubs. Discover local produce, unique gifts, and delicious treats as you explore the market's charming passages.*

5. *Bodleian Library: The grand Bodleian Library, one of the largest libraries in the UK, is a prominent feature of the city*

center. While some sections are accessible only to scholars, guided tours provide a glimpse into its fascinating history and architectural splendor.

6. Sheldonian Theatre: Designed by Christopher Wren, the Sheldonian Theatre is a magnificent venue for concerts, lectures, and university ceremonies. Take a guided tour to learn about its history and enjoy the breathtaking view from the cupola.

7. University of Oxford Colleges: The city center is home to several of the University of Oxford's historic colleges. Christ

Church College, with its impressive Tom Tower, is a highlight. Explore the college grounds, visit the cathedral, and see the dining hall that inspired Hogwarts in the Harry Potter films.

8. *Ashmolean Museum: Situated on Beaumont Street, the Ashmolean Museum is the oldest public museum in the UK. It houses a vast collection of art and artifacts, covering ancient civilizations, European masters, Eastern art, and more. Explore its galleries to discover treasures from around the world.*

9. *Museum of the History of Science: Located on Broad Street, the Museum of the History of Science showcases the history of scientific instruments and discoveries. It features exhibits on astronomy, mathematics, chemistry, and early medical instruments. Marvel at historical artifacts and learn about groundbreaking scientific achievements.*

10. *Parks and Gardens: The city center offers several green spaces where you can relax and enjoy nature. The University Parks provide a tranquil retreat along the River Cherwell, while Christ Church Meadow offers picturesque views of the college and the river.*

11.	*Shopping: In addition to the Covered Market and High Street, Oxford City Center boasts a diverse range of shops and boutiques. Explore Cornmarket Street, Queen Street, and the Clarendon Centre for a mix of well-known brands, independent stores, and specialty shops.*

12.	*Dining and Entertainment: The city center offers a wide variety of dining options, ranging from traditional British pubs to international cuisine and fine dining establishments. You'll also find theaters, cinemas, and live music venues to enjoy in the evenings.*

Oxford City Center is a captivating destination that seamlessly blends history, culture, and a vibrant atmosphere. Whether you're exploring its renowned landmarks, perusing its shops, or enjoying its culinary delights, you're sure to have a memorable experience in this captivating part of Oxford.

UNIVERSITY OF OXFORD

The University of Oxford is one of the most prestigious and oldest universities in the world, located in the city of Oxford, England. Founded in the 12th century, it has a rich history and a reputation for academic excellence.

1. *History and Prestige: The University of Oxford traces its roots back to the late 11th century, making it one of the oldest universities in the English-speaking world. It has a long-standing reputation for academic achievement, producing numerous renowned scholars, scientists, writers, and world leaders throughout its history.*

2. *Collegiate System: The University of Oxford operates on a unique collegiate system, consisting of 38 colleges and six permanent private halls. Each college is an independent institution with its own buildings, accommodation, dining halls, libraries, and academic staff. This system fosters a close-knit*

academic and social community within the larger university.

3. *Academic Excellence: The university is known for its academic rigor and high standards. It offers a wide range of disciplines and programs across various faculties, including the humanities, social sciences, natural sciences, medicine, law, and more. Oxford is consistently ranked among the top universities globally.*

4. *Libraries: The University of Oxford boasts an extensive library system, which includes the iconic Bodleian Library, one of the largest and oldest libraries*

in Europe. The Bodleian Library houses millions of books, manuscripts, and other valuable resources, making it a hub of academic research and scholarship.

5. *Colleges and Architecture: The university's colleges are renowned for their stunning architecture, which spans different time periods and architectural styles. Each college has its own distinct character and history. Prominent examples include Christ Church College, Magdalen College, and University College, to name just a few.*

6. *Notable Alumni: The University of Oxford has produced numerous notable alumni who have made significant contributions to various fields. These include world leaders like former British Prime Ministers Tony Blair and David Cameron, writers such as J.R.R. Tolkien and Oscar Wilde, scientists like Stephen Hawking, and Nobel laureates in various disciplines.*

7. *Tutorial System: One of Oxford's unique features is its tutorial system. Undergraduates often have one-on-one or small-group tutorials with academic experts, allowing for close interaction, in-depth discussions, and personalized learning. This*

system fosters critical thinking, intellectual development, and academic independence.

8. *Research Opportunities: The University of Oxford is a vibrant center for research and innovation. It attracts top researchers from around the world and offers numerous research opportunities and facilities across various disciplines. Students and scholars have access to state-of-the-art laboratories, research centers, and collaborative networks.*

9. *Cultural and Extracurricular Activities: Oxford offers a rich*

*and diverse range of
extracurricular activities, clubs,
and societies, catering to various
interests. Students can engage in
sports, music, drama,
journalism, debate, and more.
The city of Oxford itself has a
vibrant cultural scene, with
theaters, museums, literary
festivals, and other events
throughout the year.*

*10.   Influence on Oxford City:
The University of Oxford has had
a profound influence on the city
of Oxford. Many of its colleges,
libraries, and academic buildings
are integral parts of the city's
architectural landscape. The
university also contributes to the
local economy, culture, and
intellectual vibrancy of Oxford.*

107

The University of Oxford is a globally renowned institution that continues to uphold its tradition of academic excellence, research innovation, and intellectual curiosity. It offers a unique educational experience, fostering intellectual growth, personal development, and a lifelong connection to a prestigious academic community.

OXFORD COLLEGES

Oxford University is renowned for its collegiate system, which consists of 38 colleges and six permanent private halls. Each college is an independent institution with its own unique history, architecture, academic staff, and facilities.

1. *Christ Church: One of the largest and most famous colleges, Christ Church boasts stunning architecture, including Tom Tower and the Great Hall, which inspired the Great Hall in the Harry Potter films. It has a rich history and notable alumni, including Lewis Carroll.*

2. *Magdalen College: Known for its picturesque setting and beautiful deer park, Magdalen College features a stunning chapel and a tower with breathtaking views of Oxford. It has a strong musical tradition with the world-renowned choir.*

3. *University College: The oldest college in Oxford, University College, commonly known as "Univ," has a rich history dating back to the 13th century. It has notable alumni, including Bill Clinton and Stephen Hawking.*

4. *Balliol College: Balliol College is known for its academic excellence and progressive*

values. It has a reputation for producing many prominent politicians, philosophers, and writers, including Adam Smith and Aldous Huxley.

5. *St John's College: With its beautiful gardens and grand architecture, St John's College is one of the largest colleges. It has a strong academic reputation and notable alumni, including Tony Blair and Aung San Suu Kyi.*

6. *Brasenose College: Brasenose College, or "BNC," is known for its welcoming and friendly atmosphere. It has a picturesque quad and a notable rowing tradition.*

7. *Hertford College: Hertford College is situated in the heart of Oxford and known for its bridge over the Cherwell River. It has a diverse community and a reputation for academic excellence.*

8. *Oriel College: Oriel College is one of the oldest colleges and has an impressive architectural façade. It has produced notable alumni, including Cecil Rhodes and J.R.R. Tolkien.*

9. *Pembroke College: Pembroke College has a picturesque setting*

and beautiful gardens. It has a strong academic reputation and notable alumni, including Samuel Johnson and J.R.R. Tolkien.

10. Worcester College: Worcester College is known for its serene gardens and lake. It has a strong academic and sporting tradition.

11. Lady Margaret Hall: One of the first women's colleges, Lady Margaret Hall is known for its commitment to social justice and equality. It has notable alumni, including Indira Gandhi and Benazir Bhutto.

12.   Somerville College: Another pioneering women's college, Somerville College has a commitment to academic excellence and social progress. It has notable alumni, including Margaret Thatcher and Dorothy Hodgkin.

13.   Trinity College: Trinity College is known for its beautiful gardens and tranquil environment. It has notable alumni, including physicist Sir Isaac Newton.

14.   St Catherine's College: St Catherine's College, also known as "Catz," has a modern architectural style and a

*reputation for its strong
academic programs.*

*15.   New College: New College,
founded in 1379, has a beautiful
cloister and chapel. It is known
for its choir, which has a long-
standing tradition of excellence.*

*16.   Jesus College: Jesus
College has a peaceful and
secluded atmosphere, with
beautiful gardens and a lake. It
is known for its strong academic
programs and vibrant student
community.*

*17.   Wadham College: Wadham
College is known for its*

progressive values and social activism. It has a diverse and inclusive community and offers a range of academic disciplines.

18.   *Lincoln College: Lincoln College has a charming and historic setting, with its medieval buildings and picturesque quads. It is known for its strong tutorial system and academic support.*

19.   *St. Edmund Hall: St. Edmund Hall, known as "Teddy Hall," is one of the smaller colleges. It has a close-knit community and a reputation for its friendly and inclusive atmosphere.*

20.   St. Anne's College: St. Anne's College was one of the first women's colleges to be established at Oxford. It has a modern and progressive environment and offers a wide range of academic subjects.

21.   Mansfield College: Mansfield College is known for its commitment to social justice and equality. It has a strong reputation in subjects like politics, international relations, and sociology.

22.   St. Hugh's College: St. Hugh's College, founded in 1886, has a diverse and international student body. It offers a range of

117

subjects and has notable alumni, including Aung San Suu Kyi.

23.   *Exeter College: Exeter College, founded in 1314, has a mix of historic and modern buildings. It offers a wide range of academic disciplines and is known for its tutorial system.*

24.   *Corpus Christi College: Corpus Christi College has a beautiful and tranquil setting, with its secluded gardens and courtyards. It offers a range of subjects and has a strong academic reputation.*

25.   *Green Templeton College:
Green Templeton College is a
graduate college that focuses on
interdisciplinary research and
professional development. It has
a modern and innovative
approach to education.*

26.   *St. Peter's College: St.
Peter's College is known for its
friendly and welcoming
community. It offers a range of
academic subjects and has a
strong emphasis on intellectual
curiosity.*

27.   *Wolfson College: Wolfson
College is a graduate college with
a diverse and international
community. It offers a range of*

research opportunities and has a focus on interdisciplinary studies.

28. Kellogg College: Kellogg College is a graduate college that specializes in part-time and mature student education. It offers flexible study options and has a strong emphasis on professional development.

29. Blackfriars Hall: Blackfriars Hall is a permanent private hall that is home to the Dominican friars. It offers programs in philosophy and theology.

30. Keble College: Keble College is known for its striking

redbrick buildings and magnificent chapel. It has a strong reputation in the humanities and sciences.

These colleges, along with the others in the University of Oxford, contribute to the rich academic and social tapestry of the institution. Each college has its own distinct character, traditions, and contributions to the academic and cultural life of the university. They provide a supportive and stimulating environment for students, fostering intellectual growth, personal development, and a sense of belonging within the larger Oxford community.

MUSEUMS AND GALLERIES

Oxfordshire, the county in which the city of Oxford is located, is home to several notable museums and galleries. Museums and galleries in Oxfordshire:

1. *Ashmolean Museum: Located in the heart of Oxford, the Ashmolean Museum is one of the oldest and most renowned museums in the world. It houses a vast collection of art and artifacts from various civilizations, including ancient Egypt, Greece, Rome, and Asia. The museum also features works from renowned artists such as*

122

Michelangelo, Rembrandt, and Turner.

2. *Pitt Rivers Museum: Situated within the University of Oxford's Museum of Natural History, the Pitt Rivers Museum is known for its extensive collection of archaeological and ethnographic objects. It showcases artifacts from around the world, including tools, weapons, costumes, and religious objects, offering insights into human culture and history.*

3. *Museum of Natural History: Also located in Oxford, the Museum of Natural History is famous for its impressive display of natural*

123

history specimens. It houses a diverse range of exhibits, including dinosaur skeletons, fossils, minerals, and taxidermy displays. The museum is renowned for its stunning Victorian Gothic architecture.

4. *Oxford University Museum of the History of Science: This museum is dedicated to the history of science, showcasing a vast collection of scientific instruments and artifacts. It presents the evolution of scientific knowledge and discoveries, including instruments used by famous scientists like Albert Einstein and Robert Boyle.*

5. *Modern Art Oxford: As a contemporary art space, Modern Art Oxford hosts exhibitions and events showcasing innovative and thought-provoking contemporary art from both established and emerging artists. It offers a platform for artistic experimentation, dialogue, and engagement with contemporary issues.*

6. *The Oxfordshire Museum: Located in Woodstock, The Oxfordshire Museum explores the history and culture of the county. It houses a diverse collection of objects, including archaeological finds, art, and historical artifacts. The museum provides insights into the local heritage and offers*

interactive exhibits suitable for all ages.

7. *Soldiers of Oxfordshire Museum: Situated in Woodstock, this museum focuses on the military history of Oxfordshire and the stories of soldiers associated with the county. It features exhibits, artifacts, and personal testimonies, providing a deeper understanding of the impact of war on the region.*

8. *River & Rowing Museum: Located in Henley-on-Thames, the River & Rowing Museum celebrates the history, culture, and natural environment of the River Thames and the sport of rowing. It*

showcases displays on the river's ecology, the history of rowing, and temporary art exhibitions.

9. Chipping Norton Museum: This community museum in Chipping Norton offers insights into the town's history and local heritage. It features exhibits on diverse topics, including industry, agriculture, and notable individuals associated with the area.

10. Witney & District Museum: Situated in Witney, this museum tells the story of the town's history, industries, and people. It offers displays on the blanket-

making industry, local trade, and community life.

11.   *Banbury Museum: Located in Banbury, this museum explores the local history and culture of the town. It features exhibits on the town's role in the English Civil War, the famous nursery rhyme "Ride a Cock Horse," and the local industries of the past.*

12.   *Bate Collection of Musical Instruments: Housed in the Faculty of Music at the University of Oxford, the Bate Collection is one of the most important collections of musical instruments in the world. It includes a wide range of*

instruments from different periods and cultures, providing insights into the history and development of music.

13. *Oxford Museum of the History of Science: This museum, located in the original building of the Ashmolean Museum, focuses specifically on the history of scientific instruments. It showcases a remarkable collection of scientific instruments, including telescopes, microscopes, and early calculators.*

14. *Museum of Oxford: Situated in the Town Hall, the Museum of Oxford tells the story*

of the city's rich history and its people. It covers various aspects, such as the development of the city, social history, arts, and culture, through a range of displays and exhibitions.

15.   *Oxfordshire Railway Museum: Located in Didcot, this museum is dedicated to the history and preservation of railway heritage in Oxfordshire. Visitors can explore vintage locomotives, carriages, and other railway artifacts, gaining insights into the region's railway history.*

16.   *Vale and Downland Museum: Situated in Wantage, this museum focuses on the*

history, archaeology, and culture
of the Vale of White Horse. It
features exhibits on local
geology, prehistory, and notable
figures associated with the area,
such as King Alfred the Great.

17.   Chinnor and Princes
Risborough Railway: While not a
traditional museum, this heritage
railway offers visitors the chance
to experience the magic of steam
locomotives and vintage train
travel. The railway operates
along a scenic route in the
Chiltern Hills, providing a
nostalgic journey through the
countryside.

18.   Charlbury Museum:
Located in Charlbury, this
museum showcases the history
and heritage of the town and
surrounding area. It features
exhibits on local industries, rural
life, and notable events that
have shaped the community.

19.   Thame Museum: Situated
in Thame, this museum explores
the history and development of
the market town. It offers
displays on the town's historic
buildings, local trades, and the
impact of the English Civil War.

20.   Wallingford Museum:
Housed in a medieval building,
the Wallingford Museum tells the

story of the town's past. It covers various themes, including the Anglo-Saxon period, the medieval town, and the impact of the River Thames on Wallingford's history.

These museums and galleries in Oxfordshire provide visitors with a diverse range of educational and cultural experiences. Whether you have an interest in art, history, science, or local heritage, there are numerous opportunities to explore and learn about the rich tapestry of Oxfordshire's past and present. From ancient artifacts to contemporary art exhibitions, each institution offers a unique perspective on the region's history, culture, and creativity.

BOTANIC GARDEN

Oxford is home to the University of Oxford Botanic Garden, one of the oldest botanic gardens in the world and a significant attraction in the city.

History and Significance:

1. *Establishment: The University of Oxford Botanic Garden was founded in 1621, making it one of the oldest botanic gardens in the world. It was established as a physic garden, primarily for the study and cultivation of medicinal plants.*

2. *Purpose: The garden played a crucial role in the study of medicinal plants during its early years. It provided a valuable resource for physicians and scholars who sought to understand the properties and uses of various plants.*

3. *Academic Importance: The Botanic Garden has been closely connected to the University of Oxford since its inception. It serves as an educational and research facility for students, academics, and researchers studying botanical sciences.*

Features and Collections:

135

4. *Plant Collections: The Botanic Garden boasts a diverse collection of plants, including over 5,000 species. These plants are organized into various sections, such as the Medicinal Plant Collection, Taxonomic Beds, Woodland, Herbaceous Borders, and Glasshouses.*

5. *Glasshouses: The garden features a range of glasshouses that create different climatic conditions to accommodate plants from various regions and habitats. These include the Tropical House, Arid House, and Alpine House, each housing plants adapted to specific environments.*

6. *Medicinal Plant Collection: Reflecting its origins as a physic garden, the Botanic Garden maintains a dedicated collection of medicinal plants. This collection showcases a wide array of plants used historically and in modern medicine, highlighting their therapeutic properties.*

7. *Taxonomic Beds: The garden includes taxonomic beds that display plants grouped by their botanical families. This arrangement allows for the study of plant classification and provides an opportunity to observe the diversity within each family.*

8. *Walled Garden and Herbaceous Borders: The Walled Garden is a serene area within the Botanic Garden, featuring beautiful flower beds, lawns, and paths. The Herbaceous Borders showcase an array of vibrant and seasonal herbaceous plants, providing a colorful display throughout the year.*

9. *Woodland and Water Features: The Botanic Garden incorporates a woodland area, which provides a natural setting for native and shade-loving plants. Additionally, the garden features water features such as ponds, streams, and a rock garden, which enhance the overall beauty and ecological diversity.*

Research and Conservation:

10.   *Research Facilities: The Botanic Garden serves as a research hub for botanical studies, providing resources and support for various research projects. It contributes to scientific advancements and the understanding of plant biology, ecology, and conservation.*

11.   *Conservation Efforts: The garden actively participates in plant conservation initiatives, including the preservation of endangered and rare plant species. It collaborates with other institutions and organizations to safeguard plant*

139

*diversity and protect threatened
ecosystems.*

12.   Education and Outreach:

The Botanic Garden offers educational
programs, workshops, and guided
tours for visitors of all ages. These
initiatives aim to promote botanical
knowledge, environmental awareness,
and an appreciation for plant diversity.

Visitor Experience:

*13.   Accessibility: The Botanic
Garden is open to the public,
allowing visitors to explore its
collections and enjoy the
tranquility of the surroundings. It
offers accessible paths and*

140

facilities to accommodate visitors with disabilities.

14.   Events and Exhibitions: The garden hosts various events, exhibitions, and seasonal displays throughout the year. These include plant sales, art exhibitions, themed showcases, and festivals, adding to the visitor experience and providing educational opportunities.

15.   Café and Shop: The Botanic Garden features a café where visitors can relax and enjoy refreshments amidst the beautiful surroundings. There is also a shop offering a selection of

plants, gardening books, and botanical-themed gifts.

The University of Oxford Botanic Garden offers an immersive experience for visitors, combining scientific research, educational programs, and a serene environment to appreciate the beauty and importance of plants. With its rich history, diverse plant collections, and commitment to conservation, the Botanic Garden in Oxford continues to be a significant center for botanical knowledge and public engagement.

PUNTING ON THE RIVER CHERWELL

Punting on the River Cherwell is a popular recreational activity in Oxford, England. Punting involves propelling a flat-bottomed boat, known as a punt, along the river using a long pole. Punting on the River Cherwell:

Punting:

1. *History: Punting has a long history in Oxford and is closely associated with the city's university culture. Punting originated as a means of transportation and was later adopted as a leisure activity.*

2. *The Punt: A punt is a flat-bottomed boat typically made of*

wood or fiberglass. It has a
square or rectangular shape,
with a shallow draft allowing it to
navigate shallow waters. Punting
involves standing at the rear of
the punt and propelling it
forward by pushing against the
riverbed with a long pole.

3. River Cherwell: The River
   Cherwell is a picturesque river
   that flows through Oxford and is
   a tributary of the River Thames.
   It is known for its tranquil and
   scenic surroundings, making it
   an ideal location for punting.

4. Punting Experience: Punting on
   the River Cherwell offers a
   unique and leisurely way to

explore the city and its natural beauty. It allows visitors to enjoy the serenity of the river, passing under charming bridges and past lush green meadows.

5. *Self-Punting or Chauffeured Punts: There are two options for punting on the River Cherwell. Visitors can choose to self-punt, where they rent a punt and navigate the river themselves, or opt for a chauffeured punt, where a skilled punter guides the boat while providing commentary about the surroundings and points of interest.*

6. *Scenic Highlights: Punting on the River Cherwell provides*

opportunities to admire various landmarks and scenic spots, including:

- *Magdalen Bridge: This iconic bridge spanning the Cherwell offers beautiful views and is a popular spot for punting.*

- *University Parks: The river passes through the University Parks, a picturesque parkland that provides a tranquil setting for punting.*

- *Christ Church Meadow: Punting along the Cherwell allows glimpses of the scenic Christ Church Meadow, a vast green space with grazing cattle and historic buildings.*

- *Botanic Garden: The University of Oxford Botanic Garden is located near the Cherwell, and punting provides a unique perspective of the garden's riverside areas.*

7. *Season and Timing: Punting on the River Cherwell is generally available from spring to autumn, as weather and river conditions*

permit. It is advisable to check with local punt hire companies for specific operating hours and availability.

8. *Punting Tours and Hire Companies: There are several punting tour operators and punt hire companies along the River Cherwell in Oxford. These companies offer a range of services, including self-punting, chauffeured punting, and guided tours that provide historical and cultural insights.*

Punting on the River Cherwell offers a delightful and leisurely way to explore the scenic beauty of Oxford. Whether self-punting or opting for a chauffeured punt, visitors can experience the tranquility of the river, admire iconic landmarks, and immerse themselves in the unique charm of this centuries-old tradition.

SHOPPING AND DINING

Oxfordshire, located in South East England, offers a diverse range of shopping and dining experiences. From bustling city centers to charming market towns and picturesque villages, the county provides numerous options for visitors and residents alike.

Shopping:

1. *Oxford City Centre: The city of Oxford is renowned for its shopping scene, offering a mix of high-street brands, independent boutiques, and designer stores. Popular shopping destinations include Cornmarket Street, Queen Street, and the Westgate Oxford shopping center.*

2. *Bicester Village: Located just outside of Oxford, Bicester Village is a luxury shopping destination featuring over 160 designer outlet boutiques. It offers discounted prices on fashion, accessories, homeware, and more.*

3. *Covered Markets: Oxford boasts two historic covered markets, the Oxford Covered Market and the Covered Market in Abingdon. These vibrant indoor markets house a variety of stalls selling fresh produce, local delicacies, crafts, antiques, and unique gifts.*

4. *Market Towns: Several charming market towns in Oxfordshire, such as Witney, Wantage, and Thame, offer a mix of independent shops, antique stores, and regular market days where you can find fresh produce, clothing, arts, and crafts.*

5. *Independent Boutiques and Galleries: Throughout the county, you'll find numerous independent boutiques, art galleries, and craft shops offering unique products, including artisanal crafts, handmade jewelry, vintage clothing, and local artwork.*

6. *Farm Shops and Delis: Oxfordshire is known for its agricultural heritage, and many farms in the county have their own farm shops and delis. These establishments offer locally sourced produce, including fresh fruits and vegetables, meats, dairy products, and homemade delicacies.*

Dining:

1. *Oxford Dining Scene: Oxford offers a vibrant dining scene with a wide range of cuisines and culinary styles. From traditional British fare to international flavors, visitors can find restaurants, cafes, and pubs to suit every taste and budget.*

2. *Michelin-Starred Restaurants: Oxfordshire boasts several Michelin-starred restaurants, including The Nut Tree Inn in Murcott, The Sir Charles Napier in Chinnor, and The Oxford Kitchen in Oxford. These establishments offer exceptional dining experiences with top-notch cuisine and service.*

3. *Traditional Pubs and Gastropubs: Throughout the county, you'll find traditional pubs and gastropubs serving classic pub food and locally brewed ales. These establishments often feature cozy interiors, beer gardens, and a warm and friendly atmosphere.*

4. Riverside Dining: With the River Thames running through Oxfordshire, there are numerous riverside restaurants and cafes that offer picturesque views while enjoying a meal. Places such as The Trout Inn in Wolvercote and The Folly in Oxford are popular choices.

5. Afternoon Tea: Oxfordshire is known for its delightful afternoon tea offerings. Many tearooms, cafes, and hotels provide traditional afternoon tea experiences, complete with finger sandwiches, scones, cakes, and a selection of teas.

6. *Food Festivals and Farmers' Markets: Throughout the year, Oxfordshire hosts various food festivals and farmers' markets, celebrating local produce, artisanal products, and international cuisines. These events provide an opportunity to sample and purchase a wide range of delicious food and drink.*

Whether you're looking for a shopping spree in Oxford's city center, exploring the markets in charming towns, or indulging in culinary delights, Oxfordshire offers a diverse and enjoyable shopping and dining experience. From high-street brands to independent boutiques, traditional pubs to Michelin-starred restaurants, the county caters to a wide range of tastes and preferences.

HISTORIC SITES AND LANDMARKS

Oxfordshire is home to a wealth of historic sites and landmarks that showcase its rich heritage. One iconic landmark is the University of Oxford, with its stunning architecture and globally renowned academic history. Visitors can explore the college courtyards, visit the Bodleian Library, and admire the Radcliffe Camera and the Sheldonian Theatre.

Another must-see is the Ashmolean Museum, which houses an impressive collection of art and artifacts that span centuries of history. The museum offers a fascinating glimpse into the region's cultural and artistic evolution.

157

For literary enthusiasts, the Eagle and Child pub holds special significance as the meeting place of the Inklings, a literary group that included J.R.R. Tolkien and C.S. Lewis. The pub's historic ambience provides a unique opportunity to connect with Oxfordshire's literary legacy.

Beyond Oxford, travelers can discover the stunning Blenheim Palace, a UNESCO World Heritage site that boasts breathtaking architecture and beautiful gardens. This historic estate is a testament to the region's grandeur and is a delight to explore.

BLENHEIM PALACE

Blenheim Palace is a magnificent country house located in Woodstock, Oxfordshire, England. It is a UNESCO World Heritage site and one of the most iconic and grandest palaces in the country.

History:

1. *Construction: Blenheim Palace was built in the early 18th century as a gift from Queen Anne to John Churchill, the first Duke of Marlborough, in*

recognition of his military triumphs. Construction began in 1705 and took over 20 years to complete.

2. Architectural Significance: The palace was designed by renowned architect Sir John Vanbrugh in the Baroque style. It is considered a masterpiece of English architecture and is known for its grand proportions, intricate detailing, and commanding presence.

3. Birthplace of Sir Winston Churchill: Blenheim Palace holds historical significance as the birthplace of Sir Winston Churchill, one of the most

influential British statesmen and prime ministers. A dedicated exhibition explores Churchill's life and legacy within the palace.

Key Features:

4. *Palace Interiors: Blenheim Palace features opulent interiors, including the State Rooms, which showcase exquisite craftsmanship, lavish furnishings, and important artworks. Visitors can explore the Great Hall, Long Library, Saloon, and other beautifully appointed rooms.*

5. *Gardens and Parkland: The palace is surrounded by expansive gardens and parkland designed by renowned landscaper Capability Brown. The*

gardens feature formal elements, such as the Water Terraces and Italian Garden, as well as serene lakes, woodland walks, and sweeping lawns.

6. *Churchill Exhibition: The palace houses a permanent exhibition dedicated to Sir Winston Churchill. It provides insight into his life, achievements, and personal mementos, including letters, photographs, and the room where he was born.*

Visitor Experience:

7. *Tours: Guided tours are available to explore the palace's interior, including the State Rooms and the Churchill Exhibition.*

*Knowledgeable guides offer
historical context and share
stories about the palace's
grandeur and its illustrious
residents.*

8. *Park and Gardens: Visitors can
   enjoy leisurely walks through the
   extensive parkland and gardens
   surrounding the palace. The
   grounds offer picturesque vistas,
   serene lakes, and beautifully
   manicured areas, perfect for a
   peaceful retreat.*

9. *Events and Activities: Blenheim
   Palace hosts a variety of events
   and activities throughout the
   year. These include concerts,
   outdoor theater performances,*

*garden tours, and seasonal
celebrations, such as Christmas
lights displays and festive
markets.*

10.   *Formal Dining and Cafés:
The palace offers dining options,
including the elegant Orangery
Restaurant, which serves a range
of dishes using locally sourced
ingredients. There are also cafés
and tea rooms where visitors can
enjoy refreshments and light
meals.*

11.   *Gift Shop: A gift shop is
available on-site, offering a wide
selection of souvenirs, books,
artwork, and products inspired
by the palace and its history.*

Blenheim Palace is not only a historic landmark but also a vibrant cultural destination. Its stunning architecture, lush gardens, and significant connections to Winston Churchill make it a must-visit attraction in Oxfordshire. Whether exploring the palace interiors, strolling through the parkland, or learning about Churchill's life, visitors can immerse themselves in the grandeur and heritage of this remarkable palace.

CHRIST CHURCH CATHEDRAL

Christ Church Cathedral, also known as the Cathedral Church of Christ in Oxford, is a renowned religious and architectural landmark located in the heart of Oxford, England. It is both the cathedral of the Diocese of Oxford and the chapel of Christ Church College, one of the constituent colleges of the University of Oxford.

History:

1. *Foundation: The cathedral has a rich history dating back over 1,000 years. It was founded as a monastic church in the late 11th century by St. Frideswide, the patron saint of Oxford. The original church was rebuilt and expanded over the centuries into*

the magnificent structure seen today.

2. *College Connection:* Since the 16th century, the cathedral has been closely associated with Christ Church College, which was established on the same grounds. The college and cathedral share the same foundation and many architectural features, creating a unique dual-purpose space.

3. *Architectural Significance:* Christ Church Cathedral features a combination of architectural styles, including Norman, Gothic, and Renaissance elements. Its impressive spire, intricate

167

stonework, and stunning stained glass windows contribute to its visual grandeur.

Key Features:

4. Nave and Choir: The cathedral's nave is a vast and impressive space with high ceilings, stone columns, and intricate woodwork. The choir, located in the eastern part of the cathedral, is known for its beautiful stalls and intricate carvings.

5. Great Tom: The Great Tom, a bell located in the tower of Christ Church Cathedral, is one of the oldest and heaviest bells in England. It tolls 101 times each evening, a tradition that dates back to the 17th century.

6. *Stained Glass: The cathedral houses a remarkable collection of stained glass windows that depict biblical scenes, religious figures, and historical events. Notable examples include the Great East Window, the Becket Window, and the Latin American Window.*

7. *Tom Tower: The iconic Tom Tower, designed by Sir Christopher Wren, stands at the entrance to Christ Church College and serves as one of the main landmarks of the cathedral. It features a clock and a statue of the college's founder, Cardinal Thomas Wolsey.*

Visitor Experience:

8. *Worship and Services: As an active place of worship, Christ Church Cathedral holds regular services, including daily prayers, choral evensong, and Sunday worship. Visitors are welcome to attend these services and experience the spiritual atmosphere.*

9. *Guided Tours: Guided tours of the cathedral are available, providing insights into its history, architecture, and notable features. Knowledgeable guides offer commentary on the cathedral's significance within the context of Oxford's religious and academic heritage.*

10.   *Music and Choir: The cathedral is renowned for its musical tradition, with a choir that dates back centuries. Visitors may have the opportunity to hear the choir perform during services or special concerts and recitals.*

11.   *Gardens and Meadows: Adjacent to the cathedral and college, there are beautiful gardens and meadows that visitors can explore. These green spaces provide a tranquil setting and offer views of the cathedral's stunning architecture.*

12.   Connections to Literature and Film: Christ Church Cathedral and College have been featured in various literary works and films, including Lewis Carroll's "Alice's Adventures in Wonderland" and its film adaptations. Visitors can discover the connections to these cultural references while exploring the cathedral.

Christ Church Cathedral stands as a significant religious and cultural site in the city of Oxford. With its architectural splendor, historical importance, and role as a place of worship, it attracts visitors from around the world who seek to appreciate its beauty, learn about its heritage, and experience the spiritual ambiance within its walls.

172

BODLEIAN LIBRARY

The Bodleian Library is one of the oldest and most prestigious libraries in the world, located in Oxford, England. It is part of the University of Oxford's library system and serves as the main research library for the university.

History:

1. *Foundation: The library was founded in 1602 through the donation of books by Sir Thomas Bodley, a diplomat and scholar. Bodley's vision was to create a library that would be a center of learning and knowledge.*

2. *Architectural Development: Over the centuries, the Bodleian Library has undergone numerous*

expansions and renovations. Notable additions include the Radcliffe Camera in the 18th century and the Weston Library in the 21st century, which expanded the library's capacity and modernized its facilities.

Key Features:

3. *Collections: The Bodleian Library houses a vast collection of books, manuscripts, maps, prints, and other materials. It holds over 13 million printed items, including rare and valuable works, making it one of the largest libraries in the United Kingdom.*

4. *Bodleian Library Complex: The library complex consists of*

several buildings, including the historic Old Bodleian Library, the Radcliffe Camera, the Clarendon Building, the Weston Library, and various specialized libraries. Each building has its own unique architectural style and houses different collections.

5. *Radcliffe Camera: The Radcliffe Camera is an iconic circular building that serves as a reading room for the Bodleian Library. It is known for its distinctive dome and houses important collections of books and manuscripts.*

6. *Divinity School: The Divinity School, located within the Bodleian Library complex, is a*

stunning medieval building renowned for its intricate vaulted ceiling. It was originally used for theological teaching and examinations and now serves as a venue for special events and exhibitions.

Visitor Experience:

7. *Tours: Guided tours are available for visitors to explore the Bodleian Library complex and learn about its history, architecture, and collections. These tours provide access to the public areas and offer insights into the library's significance as an academic and cultural institution.*

8. *Exhibition Spaces: The library regularly hosts exhibitions that showcase its treasures and highlight specific themes or periods from its collections. These exhibitions often feature rare manuscripts, historic artifacts, and other significant materials.*

9. *Reader Access: While the Bodleian Library primarily serves as a research library for scholars and students, it is possible for members of the public to access certain materials by obtaining a reader's card and following the library's rules and regulations.*

10.   *Gift Shops: The Bodleian Library has gift shops where visitors can purchase books, souvenirs, and other items related to the library and its collections. These shops offer a wide range of products, including replicas of historic manuscripts and literary-themed merchandise.*

The Bodleian Library stands as an iconic symbol of scholarship and intellectual heritage. Its historic buildings, extensive collections, and ongoing commitment to research and learning make it a must-visit destination for those interested in literature, history, and academia. Whether exploring the grand reading rooms, attending an exhibition, or simply admiring the architecture, visitors can experience the rich legacy of knowledge preserved within the Bodleian Library.

ASHMOLEAN MUSEUM

The Ashmolean Museum is the oldest museum in the United Kingdom and one of the oldest public museums in the world. Located in Oxford, England, it is part of the University of Oxford and houses a diverse collection of art and artifacts from various periods and civilizations.

History:

1. Foundation: The museum was founded in 1683 through the bequest of Elias Ashmole, an antiquarian and collector. It was originally known as the Ashmolean Museum of Art and Archaeology and aimed to provide a space for the study and display of his extensive collection.

2. Architectural Development: The museum underwent significant expansions and renovations over the years. The most recent redevelopment, completed in 2009, created new galleries and improved facilities while preserving the historic character of the building.

Key Features:

3. Collections: The Ashmolean Museum houses a vast and diverse collection spanning thousands of years of human history. It encompasses a wide range of disciplines, including art, archaeology, numismatics, anthropology, and more. The collection includes sculptures, paintings, ceramics, textiles, coins, manuscripts, and other significant artifacts.

181

4. Ancient Egypt and Nubia: The museum has a notable collection of ancient Egyptian and Nubian artifacts. It includes mummies, funerary objects, statuary, and hieroglyphic inscriptions, providing insights into the rich cultural heritage of these ancient civilizations.

5. Western Art: The museum's art collection features works from various periods and artistic movements, including Renaissance, Baroque, Impressionism, and modern art. It includes masterpieces by artists such as Leonardo da Vinci, Michelangelo, Turner, Monet, and Van Gogh.

6. Eastern Art: The Ashmolean Museum has an extensive collection of art from Asia, including Chinese,

182

Japanese, Indian, and Islamic art. It showcases paintings, ceramics, textiles, and decorative arts, offering a glimpse into the artistic traditions of these cultures.

Visitor Experience:

7. Galleries and Exhibitions: The museum's galleries are organized thematically, allowing visitors to explore different periods, regions, and artistic styles. Temporary exhibitions are also held, offering in-depth explorations of specific topics or showcasing loaned works from other institutions.

8. Education and Events: The Ashmolean Museum offers educational programs, lectures, workshops, and events for visitors of all ages. These

activities aim to engage the public and provide deeper insights into the collections and the broader context of art and history.

9. Dining and Shopping: The museum has a café and a rooftop restaurant where visitors can enjoy refreshments and meals. There is also a gift shop offering a variety of books, souvenirs, and art-related products.

10. Research and Conservation: The Ashmolean Museum is actively involved in research and conservation of its collections. Scholars and experts work on projects related to the museum's artifacts, ensuring their preservation and contributing to academic knowledge.

The Ashmolean Museum offers a captivating journey through art, history, and culture. With its extensive and diverse collections, it provides visitors with opportunities to explore and appreciate the artistic achievements of civilizations from around the world. Whether you're interested in ancient civilizations, European art, or Eastern cultures, the Ashmolean Museum offers a rich and immersive experience for all.

SHELDONIAN THEATER

The Sheldonian Theatre, also referred to as the Sheldonian, is a notable architectural and cultural landmark located in Oxford, England. Designed by Sir Christopher Wren, the theater serves as the ceremonial hall of the University of Oxford and hosts various official university events.

History:

1. Construction: The Sheldonian Theatre was built between 1664 and 1669, commissioned by Gilbert Sheldon, the Vice-Chancellor of the University of Oxford at that time. It was designed by Sir Christopher Wren, who later became one of the most prominent architects in England.

2. Purpose: The theater was intended to provide a dedicated space for university ceremonies, including degree ceremonies, lectures, and concerts. It was also intended to showcase the grandeur and importance of the university.

Key Features:

3. Architectural Style: The Sheldonian Theatre is an outstanding example of Wren's architectural style, characterized by its classical elements and unique design. It blends classical and Baroque influences, with a circular shape and a distinctive cupola (domed roof) that rises above the building.

4. Exterior: The theater's exterior features intricate stone carvings, including ornate friezes, pilasters, and

187

statues. These decorative elements depict various figures from Greek and Roman mythology, as well as notable individuals associated with the university.

5. Theatre and Roof Walk: The interior of the Sheldonian Theatre consists of a large central space known as the theater, which can accommodate a significant number of people. The theater is surrounded by a colonnade, and there is a roof walk accessible through a series of staircases, offering panoramic views of Oxford's skyline.

6. Sheldonian Theatre and the University: The Sheldonian Theatre plays a crucial role in the life of the University of Oxford. It hosts degree ceremonies, including the Encaenia

(the university's annual honorary degree ceremony), as well as lectures, concerts, and other official university events.

Visitor Experience:

7. Guided Tours: Guided tours of the Sheldonian Theatre are available, allowing visitors to explore the theater's impressive architecture and learn about its history and significance. These tours often include access to the roof walk, providing a unique perspective of Oxford.

8. Special Events: The Sheldonian Theatre occasionally hosts special events, such as concerts, lectures, and exhibitions. These events may be open to the public, offering opportunities to

experience the theater's acoustics and cultural programming.

9. Souvenir Shop: The Sheldonian Theatre has a souvenir shop where visitors can purchase books, postcards, and other items related to the theater and the University of Oxford.

The Sheldonian Theatre stands as an architectural masterpiece and a symbol of the University of Oxford's rich heritage. Its stunning design, historical importance, and ongoing role as a venue for significant university events make it a must-visit attraction for those interested in Oxford's cultural and academic legacy.

OXFORD CASTLE

Oxford Castle is a historic Norman castle located in Oxford, England. It has a rich history spanning over 1,000 years and has served various purposes throughout its existence.

History:

1. Norman Castle: Oxford Castle was built in the late 11th century by Norman baron Robert D'Oyly. It was constructed as a motte-and-bailey castle, with a large mound (motte) and an enclosed courtyard (bailey) surrounded by a wooden palisade.

2. Royal Residence: In the 12th century, the castle became a royal residence and a center of governance for the region. Several medieval kings,

including Henry II and Richard the Lionheart, stayed at Oxford Castle during their reigns.

3. Prison: From the 14th century onwards, the castle was primarily used as a prison. It housed various prisoners, including political and religious offenders. Notable individuals who were imprisoned there include King David II of Scotland and the Oxford Martyrs, who were executed for their religious beliefs.

4. Decline and Restoration: Over time, the castle fell into disrepair, and by the 17th century, it was mostly abandoned. In the 18th and 19th centuries, parts of the castle were demolished or repurposed. However, efforts were made in the 20th and 21st

centuries to restore and preserve the remaining structures.

Visitor Experience:

5. Oxford Castle Unlocked: Today, Oxford Castle is a popular tourist attraction known as "Oxford Castle Unlocked." Visitors can explore the castle's complex through guided tours, which provide insights into its history, architecture, and the stories of those who lived and were imprisoned there.

6. St. George's Tower: One of the highlights of Oxford Castle is St. George's Tower, the surviving part of the medieval castle. Visitors can climb the tower and enjoy panoramic views of Oxford's skyline.

193

7. Prison D-Wing: The prison's D-Wing has been converted into a visitor attraction that offers an immersive experience, showcasing the harsh conditions prisoners faced during their time at the castle.

8. Underground Crypt: The castle's underground crypt, which dates back to the 11th century, has been restored and is open to visitors. It provides a glimpse into the castle's earliest history and architectural features.

9. Oxford Castle Quarter: The area surrounding Oxford Castle has been developed into a vibrant quarter with shops, restaurants, and a hotel. It offers a combination of historical charm and modern amenities.

Oxford Castle is a fascinating destination for history enthusiasts, offering a glimpse into the city's medieval past and the evolution of the castle over the centuries. Whether exploring the tower, descending into the crypt, or learning about the castle's role as a prison, visitors can immerse themselves in the rich heritage of Oxford Castle.

THE RADCLIFFE CAMERA

The Radcliffe Camera is a distinctive circular building located in Oxford, England. It is one of the most iconic landmarks in the city and serves as a reading room for the Bodleian Library, one of the oldest and largest libraries in Europe.

History:

1. *Construction: The Radcliffe Camera was built between 1737 and 1749. It was designed by architect James Gibbs in the Neoclassical style. The building was funded by a bequest from John Radcliffe, a physician, who left money in his will for the construction of a library.*

2. *Purpose: The Radcliffe Camera was originally intended to house the Radcliffe Science Library, which was part of the University of Oxford. However, it later became a reading room for the Bodleian Library, serving as a space for students and scholars to study and access resources.*

Architecture:

3. *Design: The Radcliffe Camera is known for its circular shape, which is a rare architectural feature. The exterior is characterized by its grandeur and classical design, with a domed roof, Corinthian columns, and ornate detailing.*

4. *Materials: The building is constructed of local limestone, giving it a distinct pale yellow color. The architectural elements, such as the columns and the dome, are made of Portland stone, which contrasts with the limestone.*

5. *Interior: The interior of the Radcliffe Camera features a central circular reading room surrounded by bookshelves. The space is beautifully designed, with natural light streaming in from the large windows and a sense of grandeur created by the high ceilings and the dome.*

Role and Access:

6. *Reading Room: The Radcliffe Camera is primarily a reading room for the Bodleian Library, providing a quiet and focused environment for studying. It houses books and periodicals from a wide range of subjects.*

7. *Bodleian Libraries: The Radcliffe Camera is part of the Bodleian Libraries system, which encompasses numerous libraries across Oxford University. It serves as an important resource for students, researchers, and academics.*

8. *Access: Access to the Radcliffe Camera is limited to registered readers of the Bodleian Libraries.*

However, the exterior of the building can be enjoyed by visitors who wish to admire its architectural beauty and take photographs.

The Radcliffe Camera stands as a symbol of scholarship and learning in Oxford. Its elegant design and central location make it a prominent landmark in the city's skyline. Whether as a functioning reading room or as an architectural marvel, the Radcliffe Camera holds a significant place in the academic and cultural life of Oxford University.

THE BRIDGE OF SIGHS

The Bridge of Sighs in Oxford is a picturesque and iconic landmark that is often associated with the city's rich history and architectural splendor. Officially known as Hertford Bridge, this historic structure connects two parts of Hertford College over New College Lane. The bridge bears a resemblance to the famous Bridge of Sighs in Venice, hence its more commonly known name.

Built in 1914, the Bridge of Sighs was designed by Sir Thomas Jackson, the renowned architect responsible for several Oxford buildings. The bridge's distinctive design features ornate stonework and large windows, creating an elegant and romantic ambiance that has made it a popular spot for visitors and photographers.

201

The term "Bridge of Sighs" is believed to have originated from the idea that the scenic view from the bridge might have elicited sighs of admiration from those crossing it. The bridge's romantic allure and architectural beauty have made it a beloved symbol of Oxford's charm and heritage.

Visitors to Oxford often seek out the Bridge of Sighs as part of their exploration of the city's historic attractions. Its proximity to other notable landmarks, such as the Bodleian Library and the Radcliffe Camera, makes it a convenient stop for those wishing to soak in the architectural and cultural splendor of Oxford.

Whether admired from afar or crossed for an up-close view of its craftsmanship, the Bridge of Sighs remains a quintessential part of Oxford's identity, embodying the city's timeless allure and historic significance.

BROUGHTON CASTLE

Broughton Castle is a historic fortified manor house located near Banbury in Oxfordshire, England. It is a picturesque and well-preserved medieval castle that has served as a residence for the Fiennes family for over 600 years.

History:

1. Construction: Broughton Castle dates back to the 14th century when it was originally constructed as a manor house. Over the centuries, it underwent various architectural additions and modifications, resulting in a unique blend of medieval and Tudor architecture.

2. Fiennes Family: The castle has been owned by the Fiennes family since the 15th century. Notable members of the family include Sir Richard Fiennes, who was a close advisor to King Henry VIII, and his descendant, the 17th-century Parliamentarian and diplomat Nathaniel Fiennes.

Key Features:

3. Architecture: Broughton Castle features a mix of architectural styles, including medieval fortified elements and Tudor domestic architecture. It has a rectangular layout with a central courtyard and is surrounded by a moat. The castle's stone walls, towers, and battlements contribute to its imposing appearance.

4. Great Hall: The castle's Great Hall is a significant architectural feature, showcasing medieval craftsmanship with its high timber ceiling, intricate carvings, and a large fireplace. It served as the main gathering space for the family and their guests.

5. Gardens and Grounds: Broughton Castle is set within beautiful gardens and landscaped grounds. The gardens feature formal lawns, herbaceous borders, rose gardens, and a walled garden. Visitors can explore the grounds and enjoy the tranquil surroundings.

Visiting Experience:

6. Guided Tours: Broughton Castle is open to the public for guided tours during specific opening times. The

206

tours provide insights into the castle's history, architecture, and the stories of the Fiennes family. Visitors can explore the Great Hall, bedrooms, and other areas of the castle.

7. Events and Venue Hire: The castle is occasionally used as a venue for weddings, private events, and cultural activities. It offers a unique and historic setting for special occasions.

Broughton Castle stands as a testament to medieval and Tudor architecture, providing visitors with a glimpse into the region's history. Its well-preserved features, including the Great Hall and beautiful gardens, make it a popular attraction for history enthusiasts and those seeking to enjoy its picturesque surroundings.

207

NATURAL BEAUTY AND OUTDOOR ACTIVITIES

The Oxfordshire region is renowned for its natural beauty and offers a wide array of outdoor activities for nature enthusiasts and adventurers alike. From rolling countryside to picturesque rivers, there are diverse landscapes to explore and enjoy.

The Cotswolds, an Area of Outstanding Natural Beauty, is a prime example of Oxfordshire's natural allure. This region is characterized by its rolling hills, charming stone villages, and meandering walking trails, providing ample opportunities for hiking, cycling, and exploring the great outdoors. Visitors can revel in the panoramic views and soak in the tranquility of this idyllic countryside.

For those with a penchant for water-based activities, the River Thames offers a picturesque backdrop for boating, punting, and riverside strolls. The serene waters and lush riverbanks create a peaceful setting for leisurely pursuits and outdoor relaxation.

Additionally, Oxfordshire is home to several expansive parks and gardens, such as the University of Oxford Botanic Garden and Blenheim Palace grounds, where visitors can bask in the splendor of meticulously manicured landscapes and vibrant floral displays.

Outdoor enthusiasts can also partake in activities such as horseback riding, wildlife spotting, and even hot air balloon rides, allowing them to fully immerse themselves in the region's natural beauty from new and exciting perspectives.

So, whether it's exploring the Cotswolds, meandering along the River Thames, or discovering the region's stunning parks and gardens, Oxfordshire offers a wealth of natural beauty and outdoor activities for all to enjoy.

COTSWOLDS AREA OF OUTSTANDING NATURAL BEAUTY

The Cotswolds is an Area of Outstanding Natural Beauty (AONB) located in south-central England, primarily spanning across the counties of Gloucestershire, Oxfordshire, Warwickshire, Wiltshire, and Worcestershire. It is renowned for its idyllic countryside, charming villages, rolling hills, and distinctive limestone architecture.

Geography and Landscape:

1. *Scenic Countryside: The Cotswolds is characterized by its beautiful rural landscapes, featuring rolling hills, meandering rivers, and picturesque valleys. The area is*

212

known for its quintessential English countryside charm and is often referred to as the "Heart of England."

2. *Limestone Hills: The Cotswolds is predominantly composed of Cotswold stone, a type of golden limestone that is prevalent in the region. The stone is used in many of the traditional buildings and architecture, giving the area its unique and recognizable appearance.*

Charming Villages and Towns:

3. *Traditional Architecture: The Cotswolds is famous for its charming villages and towns, which showcase traditional*

Cotswold stone architecture. These buildings often have thatched roofs, honey-colored facades, and distinctive features like mullioned windows and ornate doorways.

4. *Notable Villages: Some of the well-known villages within the Cotswolds include Bibury, Bourton-on-the-Water, Broadway, Chipping Campden, Lower Slaughter, and Stow-on-the-Wold. These villages are popular tourist destinations and offer visitors a glimpse into the region's history and rural life.*

Outdoor Activities and Recreation:

5. *Walking and Hiking: The Cotswolds offers an extensive network of footpaths and trails, making it a popular destination for walkers and hikers. There are routes suitable for all levels of fitness, providing opportunities to explore the countryside and enjoy breathtaking views.*

6. *Cycling: The Cotswolds is also a great place for cycling, with quiet country lanes and designated cycling routes. Visitors can hire bikes locally or bring their own to explore the scenic landscapes at their own pace.*

7. *Wildlife and Nature: The AONB is home to a diverse range of*

wildlife and habitats. Visitors may spot species such as deer, hares, birds, and butterflies. The Cotswolds also has nature reserves and parks where nature enthusiasts can observe and appreciate the local flora and fauna.

Heritage and Attractions:

8. *Historic Sites: The Cotswolds has a rich history, and there are numerous historic sites and landmarks to explore. These include ancient churches, stately homes, castles, and archaeological sites that offer insights into the area's past.*

9. *Arts, Crafts, and Culture: The Cotswolds has a vibrant arts and*

crafts scene, with many galleries, workshops, and festivals celebrating local talent and creativity. Visitors can discover traditional crafts such as pottery, glassblowing, and woodworking.

The Cotswolds AONB offers visitors a tranquil and picturesque escape, with its stunning landscapes, charming villages, and a wealth of outdoor activities. Whether you're interested in exploring historic sites, enjoying outdoor pursuits, or simply immersing yourself in the beauty of the countryside, the Cotswolds provides a memorable experience.

CHILTERN HILLS

The Chiltern Hills is an Area of Outstanding Natural Beauty (AONB)

217

located in England, stretching across parts of Buckinghamshire, Oxfordshire, Hertfordshire, and Bedfordshire. It is a picturesque and diverse landscape characterized by rolling chalk hills, beech woodlands, and charming villages.

Geography and Landscape:

1. *Chalk Hills: The Chiltern Hills are primarily composed of chalk, which gives rise to their distinctively rolling landscape. The hills are part of a chalk escarpment that stretches across the region, offering panoramic views from their summits.*

2. *Woodlands and Valleys: The Chiltern Hills are interspersed with beautiful woodlands,*

particularly beech woodlands, which provide habitat for a variety of wildlife. The valleys and dales between the hills are dotted with picturesque villages, farmland, and meandering streams.

Outdoor Activities and Recreation:

3. *Walking and Hiking: The Chiltern Hills offer a network of footpaths and trails, making it a popular destination for walkers and hikers. There are routes suitable for all abilities, ranging from gentle strolls to more challenging hikes, allowing visitors to explore the stunning landscapes and enjoy the peaceful countryside.*

4. *Cycling: The Chilterns is a great area for cycling, with quiet country lanes and designated cycling routes. Cyclists can explore the rolling hills and picturesque villages at their own pace, enjoying the scenic beauty of the countryside.*

5. *Nature and Wildlife: The Chiltern Hills are home to a rich variety of flora and fauna. The woodlands provide habitat for species such as red kites, deer, and butterflies, while the chalk grasslands are known for their wildflowers, including orchids. Several nature reserves and protected areas within the AONB allow visitors to appreciate and discover the local wildlife.*

Heritage and Attractions:

6. *Historic Sites: The Chiltern Hills are steeped in history, with numerous historic sites and landmarks to explore. There are ancient hill forts, Iron Age earthworks, medieval churches, and historic manor houses that offer insights into the region's past.*

7. *Charming Villages: The Chiltern Hills are dotted with picturesque villages and market towns, each with its own unique character and architectural charm. These villages often feature traditional cottages, thatched roofs, and welcoming country pubs, providing a glimpse into rural life*

and offering a warm welcome to visitors.

8. *Cultural Events: The Chilterns host various cultural events throughout the year, including village fairs, food festivals, and arts exhibitions. These events celebrate local traditions, crafts, and produce, providing an opportunity to experience the vibrant community spirit of the area.*

The Chiltern Hills AONB offers visitors a scenic and tranquil escape, with its rolling hills, woodlands, and charming villages. Whether you enjoy outdoor activities, exploring historic sites, or simply immersing yourself in the beauty of the countryside, the Chiltern Hills provide a memorable experience.

RIVER THAMES

The River Thames is one of the most iconic and significant rivers in the United Kingdom. It flows through southern England, starting from its source in the Cotswolds and winding its way through London before emptying into the North Sea.

Geography and Importance:

1. *Length and Route: The River Thames spans approximately 215 miles (346 kilometers), making it the longest river entirely in England. It passes through several counties, including Gloucestershire, Oxfordshire, Berkshire, Buckinghamshire, Surrey, and Greater London.*

2. *Source and Tributaries: The Thames begins as a small stream in the Cotswolds, near the village of Kemble in Gloucestershire. Along its course, it is joined by numerous tributaries, including the Cherwell, the Wey, the Kennet, and the River Lea.*

Historical Significance:

3. *Cultural and Historical Importance: The River Thames has played a significant role in the history and culture of England. It served as a major trade route, contributing to the growth and prosperity of towns and cities along its banks. The river has been a focal point for various historical events, including the Roman occupation,*

Viking invasions, and the development of London as a global city.

4. *Bridges and Landmarks: The River Thames is spanned by numerous iconic bridges, such as Tower Bridge, London Bridge, and Westminster Bridge. These bridges are not only functional but also serve as symbols of London's identity and architectural heritage. The river is also home to notable landmarks like the Houses of Parliament, the Tower of London, and the London Eye.*

Recreational and Cultural Activities:

5. *River Cruises: The Thames is a popular destination for river cruises, offering visitors an opportunity to enjoy scenic views of the city and countryside. Cruises range from short sightseeing tours to longer excursions exploring the river's various stretches.*

6. *Rowing and Boating: The Thames has a rich tradition of rowing, with numerous rowing clubs and events taking place on its waters. The Oxford and Cambridge Boat Race, an annual rowing competition between the universities, is one of the most famous events held on the river.*

7. *Thames Path: The Thames Path is a long-distance walking trail that follows the river's course for approximately 184 miles (296 kilometers). It allows walkers to explore the diverse landscapes, historic sites, and charming towns along the river's banks.*

Environmental Importance:

8. *Wildlife and Conservation: The River Thames supports a diverse range of flora and fauna. Efforts have been made to improve water quality and restore habitats to protect and enhance the river's biodiversity. The Thames Estuary is also vital for birdlife and is designated as a Special Protection Area.*

The River Thames holds immense cultural, historical, and recreational significance. It serves as a vital transportation route, a focal point of London's skyline, and a source of enjoyment and inspiration for locals and visitors alike.

WYTHAM WOODS

Wytham Woods is a semi-natural woodland located near the village of Wytham, just northwest of Oxford in England. It is an internationally renowned ecological research site and a designated Site of Special Scientific Interest (SSSI).

Location and Size:

1. *Location: Wytham Woods is situated approximately 5 miles (8 kilometers) northwest of Oxford, within the Wytham Estate. It covers an area of about 1,000 acres (400 hectares).*

Ecological Importance:

230

2. *Research Site: Wytham Woods is widely recognized as one of the most important ecological research sites in the United Kingdom. It has a long history of ecological studies, dating back to the 1920s. The woods provide a controlled and well-documented environment for studying various aspects of ecology, including plant and animal populations, climate change, and ecosystem dynamics.*

3. *Biodiversity: The woods are home to a diverse range of flora and fauna. The woodland habitat consists primarily of deciduous trees, such as oak, beech, and ash. It supports a rich understory of wildflowers and ferns, along with a variety of fungi and*

mosses. The woods provide
habitat for numerous bird
species, mammals, insects, and
other wildlife.

Access and Conservation:

4. *Public Access: While Wytham
   Woods is primarily a research
   site, there is limited public
   access for recreation and
   education. Guided walks and
   events are occasionally organized
   to allow visitors to experience
   the natural beauty of the woods
   and learn about the ongoing
   research.*

5. *Conservation and Management:
   Wytham Woods is managed by
   the University of Oxford's*

Wytham Woods research team in collaboration with landowners and other stakeholders. The management aims to balance ecological research with the conservation of this valuable woodland habitat.

Educational and Outreach Activities:

6. *Education and Outreach: Wytham Woods plays an important role in environmental education and outreach. The research team organizes educational programs and events for schools, universities, and the general public, providing opportunities to learn about ecology, conservation, and the importance of woodland ecosystems.*

7. *Long-Term Studies: The long-term ecological research conducted at Wytham Woods has contributed to scientific knowledge and understanding of ecological processes over many decades. The data collected has been used in numerous studies and publications, informing conservation efforts and policy decisions.*

Wytham Woods is a unique woodland area that serves as a living laboratory for ecological research. Its combination of scientific significance, biodiversity, and accessibility for education and outreach make it a valuable resource for understanding and conserving woodland ecosystems.

234

WALKING AND CYCLING ROUTES

Oxfordshire offers a variety of walking and cycling routes that allow you to explore its picturesque landscapes, charming villages, and historic sites.

235

Walking Routes:

1. *The Thames Path: The Thames Path is a long-distance walking trail that follows the course of the River Thames. In Oxfordshire, you can enjoy scenic walks along the river, passing through charming towns such as Oxford, Abingdon, and Wallingford.*

2. *The Oxfordshire Way: The Oxfordshire Way is a 65-mile (105-kilometer) long-distance footpath that stretches from Bourton-on-the-Water in the Cotswolds to Henley-on-Thames. It offers a variety of landscapes, including rolling hills, woodlands, and picturesque villages.*

3. *The Chiltern Way: The Chiltern Way is a circular walking route that covers approximately 134 miles (215 kilometers) in the Chiltern Hills Area of Outstanding Natural Beauty (AONB). The trail takes you through beautiful countryside, beech woodlands, and charming Chiltern villages.*

4. *The Ridgeway National Trail: The Ridgeway is one of England's oldest trails, spanning 87 miles (139 kilometers) from the Chiltern Hills to the North Wessex Downs. It offers panoramic views, ancient historical sites, and a chance to*

walk along the rolling chalk downs.

Cycling Routes:

1. *Oxford to the Cotswolds: This cycling route takes you from Oxford into the scenic Cotswolds, passing through picturesque villages and beautiful countryside. You can explore places like Woodstock, Burford, and the stunning landscape of the Cotswolds Area of Outstanding Natural Beauty.*

2. *Oxford Canal Towpath: The Oxford Canal runs from Oxford to Coventry, and its towpath provides a pleasant cycling route. You can enjoy a leisurely*

ride along the canal, passing through peaceful countryside and charming canal-side villages.

3. *Bicester Village to Waddesdon Manor: This cycling route takes you from the famous shopping destination of Bicester Village to the stunning Waddesdon Manor. You can cycle through the countryside, enjoying the scenic beauty before reaching the grandeur of the manor.*

4. *Shotover Country Park: Shotover Country Park, located just outside Oxford, offers a network of mountain biking trails suitable for different skill levels. It provides a mix of woodland and*

*open spaces, with trails that
range from gentle to more
challenging for off-road cycling
enthusiasts.*

These are just a few examples of the walking and cycling routes available in Oxfordshire. Whether you prefer a leisurely stroll along a river or a challenging bike ride through rolling hills, Oxfordshire offers a range of options to explore its natural beauty and historic landmarks.

GARDENS AND PARKS

Oxfordshire is home to several delightful gardens and parks where you can relax, enjoy nature, and explore beautiful landscapes.

1. *University of Oxford Botanic Garden (Oxford): Located in the heart of Oxford, the University of Oxford Botanic Garden is the oldest botanic garden in the UK. It features a diverse collection of plants from around the world, including themed borders, glasshouses, and a beautiful walled garden.*

2. *Blenheim Palace and Gardens (Woodstock): Blenheim Palace is*

a UNESCO World Heritage Site and boasts stunning gardens designed by renowned landscape architect Capability Brown. The gardens feature sweeping lawns, formal flower beds, a rose garden, and a magnificent water terrace.

3. *Harcourt Arboretum (Nuneham Courtenay): Managed by the University of Oxford, Harcourt Arboretum is a tranquil woodland garden with a diverse collection of trees and shrubs. It offers beautiful trails, open meadows, and a wildflower meadow, providing a peaceful escape from the city.*

4. *Rousham House and Gardens (Bicester): Rousham House is a historic country house with breathtaking gardens designed in the 18th century. The gardens feature classical elements, including a grand avenue, temples, cascades, and a walled garden.*

5. *Waterperry Gardens (Waterperry): Waterperry Gardens is a horticultural gem known for its enchanting herbaceous borders, rose gardens, and water lily canal. The gardens also house a garden center, art galleries, and a tea room.*

6. *Buscot Park (Faringdon): Buscot Park is a stately home with extensive gardens and parkland. The gardens feature formal terraces, beautiful water features, and a famous water garden designed by Harold Peto.*

7. *Nuneham House and Gardens (Nuneham Courtenay): Nuneham House is surrounded by picturesque gardens and parkland overlooking the River Thames. The gardens offer a mix of formal and informal areas, including a walled garden, ornamental lakes, and woodlands.*

8. *Cutteslowe and Sunnymead Park (Oxford): Cutteslowe and Sunnymead Park is a popular public park in Oxford. It offers open green spaces, a lake, playgrounds, sports facilities, and a miniature steam railway.*

These are just a few examples of the gardens and parks you can explore in Oxfordshire. Each provides its own unique charm and opportunities to appreciate nature's beauty. Whether you're looking for formal gardens, peaceful woodlands, or open green spaces, Oxfordshire has something to offer for everyone.

WILDLIFE WATCHING

245

Oxfordshire offers various opportunities for wildlife watching, with its diverse habitats including woodlands, wetlands, meadows, and rivers. Here are some popular locations in Oxfordshire for observing wildlife:

1. *Otmoor RSPB Reserve: Located northeast of Oxford, Otmoor is a wetland reserve managed by the Royal Society for the Protection of Birds (RSPB). It is known for its rich birdlife, including marsh harriers, bitterns, lapwings, and reed buntings. The reserve has several walking trails and observation hides.*

2. *Chimney Meadows Nature Reserve: Situated near Bampton, Chimney Meadows is a nature*

reserve managed by the
Berkshire, Buckinghamshire, and
Oxfordshire Wildlife Trust
(BBOWT). It comprises wet
meadows, reed beds, and
ancient hedgerows. Here, you
may spot meadow birds, such as
lapwings, redshanks, curlews,
and skylarks.

3. Bernwood Meadows: Located
near Bicester, Bernwood
Meadows is a wetland reserve
managed by BBOWT. It offers a
variety of habitats, including wet
meadows, reed beds, and ponds.
The reserve is home to a range
of bird species, including
kingfishers, water rails, and
various warblers.

4. *Wytham Woods: As mentioned earlier, Wytham Woods near Oxford is an excellent location for wildlife observation. The ancient woodland is known for its diverse birdlife, including owls, woodpeckers, and various songbirds. You may also encounter mammals like deer, foxes, and squirrels.*

5. *River Thames: The River Thames and its surrounding areas provide opportunities for spotting waterfowl, such as swans, ducks, and herons. In addition, the river is home to fish species like trout and grayling. Walking or cycling along the Thames Path can offer chances to observe wildlife.*

6. *Nature Reserves and Country Parks: Oxfordshire has several other nature reserves and country parks that offer wildlife-watching opportunities. Some notable ones include Aston Rowant National Nature Reserve, Foxholes Nature Reserve, Wittenham Clumps, and Shotover Country Park.*

When wildlife watching, it is important to respect the habitats and wildlife by observing from a distance and not disturbing their natural behaviors. Binoculars, field guides, and a patient approach can enhance your wildlife-watching experience. Additionally, local wildlife organizations and visitor centers can provide information on the best times and locations for spotting specific species in Oxfordshire.

VILLAGES AND TOWNS

Oxfordshire is dotted with charming villages and towns that exude idyllic English character and offer an array of attractions for visitors to explore. From historic market towns to quaint villages nestled in picturesque landscapes, each locality boasts its own unique charm and allure.

The historic city of Oxford, with its world-renowned university, is a cultural and architectural gem, offering a blend of ancient and modern attractions. Visitors can stroll through the city's cobbled streets, visit the prestigious colleges, and marvel at iconic landmarks such as the Bodleian Library and Radcliffe Camera.

The market town of Witney is celebrated for its traditional market square, historic architecture, and vibrant community spirit. Meanwhile, the town of Woodstock is home to the magnificent Blenheim Palace, a UNESCO World Heritage Site surrounded by stunning parkland and gardens.

For a taste of quintessential village life, the Cotswolds region is replete with charming settlements like Burford, Chipping Norton, and Bourton-on-the-Water, where visitors can meander through quaint streets, admire honey-hued cottages, and partake in traditional English pastimes.

Further afield, the market town of Bicester is renowned for its designer shopping outlets at Bicester Village, while the riverside town of Abingdon-on-Thames offers historical sites, riverside walks, and a bustling town center.

Each village and town in Oxfordshire offers its own blend of history, culture, and natural beauty, providing visitors with a delightful tapestry of experiences to savor as they traverse the region's rich tapestry of localities.

WOODSTOCK

Woodstock is a historic market town located in Oxfordshire, England. The town is known for its picturesque charm, proximity to the stunning Blenheim Palace, and rich history.

Location and History:

1. *Location: Woodstock is situated about 8 miles (13 kilometers) northwest of Oxford. It is nestled in the Oxfordshire countryside and serves as a gateway to the Cotswolds.*

2. *Historic Significance: Woodstock has a long and fascinating history dating back to the 12th century. The town was originally known for its royal hunting*

lodge, which eventually became the magnificent Blenheim Palace, the birthplace of Sir Winston Churchill.

Blenheim Palace:

3. *Blenheim Palace: The grand centerpiece of Woodstock is Blenheim Palace, a UNESCO World Heritage Site. Built in the 18th century, it is one of the most impressive stately homes in England. The palace, surrounded by beautiful landscaped gardens designed by Capability Brown, is open to the public and offers tours of its opulent interiors, extensive art collections, and stunning parkland.*

Town Features:

4. *Market Square: Woodstock's Market Square is a charming area lined with historic buildings, independent shops, cafes, and restaurants. It serves as a hub for local events and markets.*

5. *St. Mary Magdalene Church: The town's parish church, St. Mary Magdalene, is a notable landmark. It dates back to the 12th century and features a distinctive spire. The church is worth visiting for its architectural beauty and historical significance.*

6. *Architecture and Streetscape: Woodstock showcases a mix of*

architectural styles, including timber-framed buildings, Georgian townhouses, and picturesque cottages. The streets are lined with shops, galleries, and inviting places to eat and drink.

Events and Festivals:

7. Woodstock Literary Festival: The town hosts an annual Woodstock Literary Festival, featuring talks, readings, and discussions by renowned authors and speakers.

8. Christmas Festival: Woodstock comes alive during the festive season with a Christmas festival that includes a lights switch-on, markets, and seasonal activities.

257

Woodstock offers a delightful blend of history, culture, and natural beauty. Whether you're exploring the majestic Blenheim Palace, strolling through the town's streets, or enjoying the nearby countryside, Woodstock provides a charming destination for visitors and locals alike.

HENLEY-ON-THAMES

Henley-on-Thames is a historic market town located in Oxfordshire, England. It is situated on the banks of the River Thames and is known for its picturesque setting, rowing heritage, and lively events.

Location and River Thames:

1. *Location: Henley-on-Thames is located approximately 8 miles (13 kilometers) northeast of Reading and 25 miles (40 kilometers) southeast of Oxford. It is nestled in the beautiful Oxfordshire countryside.*

2. *River Thames: The town's location on the River Thames is one of its defining features. The river provides a picturesque backdrop and offers opportunities for boating, river walks, and riverside picnics. Henley-on-Thames is particularly renowned for its rowing heritage and hosts the annual Henley Royal Regatta, one of the most prestigious rowing events in the world.*

Town Features:

3. *Henley Bridge: Spanning the River Thames, Henley Bridge is an iconic landmark of the town. It is a five-arched bridge that dates back to the 18th century and provides stunning views of the river and surrounding area.*

4. *Market Square: The heart of Henley-on-Thames is its Market Square, a bustling area lined with historic buildings, shops, cafes, and restaurants. The square hosts regular markets, where you can find local produce, crafts, and antiques.*

5. St. Mary's Church: St. Mary's Church is an imposing medieval church located in the center of Henley-on-Thames. It features a striking tower and beautiful stained glass windows. The church is worth a visit to appreciate its architecture and serene atmosphere.

6. Riverfront Walks and Parks: Henley-on-Thames offers scenic riverfront walks along the Thames Path, allowing you to enjoy the natural beauty of the river and its surroundings. The town also has lovely parks and green spaces, such as Mill Meadows and Marsh Meadows, where you can relax, have a picnic, or watch the river activity.

Events and Festivals:

7. *Henley Royal Regatta: The Henley Royal Regatta is a world-renowned rowing event held annually in July. It attracts rowers and spectators from around the globe, who come to watch thrilling races and enjoy the festive atmosphere along the riverbank.*

8. *Henley Festival: The Henley Festival is an annual music and arts festival held in July. It features live performances by renowned musicians, art exhibitions, fireworks, and gourmet dining experiences.*

Henley-on-Thames offers a unique blend of riverside beauty, historic charm, and vibrant events. Whether you're exploring the town's architecture, enjoying river activities, or immersing yourself in the rowing culture, Henley-on-Thames provides a wonderful destination with a distinct character.

BURFORD

Burford is a charming medieval town located in the Cotswolds, a designated Area of Outstanding Natural Beauty in Oxfordshire, England. Known for its picturesque streets, historic buildings, and scenic surroundings, Burford attracts visitors with its timeless beauty.

Location and Setting:

1. *Location: Burford is situated on the River Windrush, about 20 miles (32 kilometers) west of Oxford. It is centrally located in the Cotswolds, making it an ideal base for exploring the region's rolling hills and idyllic countryside.*

2. *Cotswold Stone Architecture:*
   Burford is famous for its
   distinctive Cotswold stone
   buildings, which feature a warm
   golden hue. The town's
   architecture showcases a mix of
   medieval, Tudor, and Georgian
   styles, with timber-framed
   houses, stone cottages, and
   elegant townhouses lining its
   narrow streets.

Town Features:

3. *High Street: The picturesque*
   High Street is the heart of
   Burford. It is lined with historic
   buildings, boutique shops, art
   galleries, antique stores, and
   traditional pubs. Strolling along

265

this charming street allows you to soak in the town's atmosphere and admire the architecture.

4. *Church of St. John the Baptist: The Church of St. John the Baptist is a prominent landmark in Burford. Known for its magnificent medieval architecture, the church features a striking spire and beautiful stained glass windows. Visitors can explore its interior and appreciate its historical and architectural significance.*

5. *Burford Priory: Located just outside the town, Burford Priory is a stunning country house with beautiful gardens. The priory has*

a rich history dating back to the 13th century and has been inhabited by notable figures throughout the centuries. The gardens are open to the public and offer a tranquil oasis with manicured lawns, herbaceous borders, and a walled garden.

6. *Wildlife and Nature: The Burford area is surrounded by scenic countryside, meandering rivers, and rolling hills. It offers opportunities for countryside walks, wildlife spotting, and enjoying the natural beauty of the Cotswolds.*

Events and Festivals:

267

7. *Cotswold Festival: Burford hosts the annual Cotswold Festival, a celebration of local arts, music, and culture. It features live performances, exhibitions, workshops, and family-friendly activities.*

8. *Christmas Market: During the festive season, Burford holds a Christmas Market with stalls selling crafts, gifts, and seasonal treats. It creates a festive atmosphere and offers a chance to find unique presents.*

Burford's timeless beauty, rich history, and idyllic location make it a popular destination in the Cotswolds. Whether you're exploring its historic streets, visiting the local landmarks, or immersing yourself in the tranquility of the surrounding countryside, Burford offers a quintessential Cotswold experience.

ABINGDON-ON-THAMES

Abingdon-on-Thames, commonly referred to as Abingdon, is a historic market town located in Oxfordshire, England. Situated on the River Thames, it is known for its rich history, picturesque setting, and cultural heritage.

Location and Setting:

1. *Location: Abingdon is situated about 6 miles (10 kilometers) south of Oxford, making it easily accessible from the city. It is located on the banks of the River Thames and is surrounded by beautiful countryside.*

2. *River Thames: The town's location on the River Thames*

provides a scenic backdrop and offers opportunities for riverside walks, boating, and enjoying the tranquil waterway.

Town Features:

3. *Market Place: The Market Place is the central square of Abingdon, bustling with activity and lined with historic buildings. It is home to a vibrant market held on certain days of the week, where you can find fresh produce, crafts, and other goods.*

4. *Abingdon Abbey: The town was historically known for its abbey, which was founded in the 7th century. Although the abbey no longer stands, you can visit the*

271

remains and the adjacent picturesque Abbey Gardens, which are perfect for a leisurely stroll.

5. *St. Helen's Church: St. Helen's Church is a notable landmark in Abingdon. Dating back to the 12th century, the church features impressive architecture, including a Norman tower and beautiful stained glass windows.*

6. *Abingdon County Hall Museum: Housed in a historic building, the Abingdon County Hall Museum showcases the town's history and heritage through displays, exhibitions, and artifacts. It provides insights into Abingdon's*

past, including its connection to the Abbey and its role as a market town.

Events and Festivals:

7. *Abingdon Traditional Morris Dancing: Abingdon is known for its traditional Morris dancing, a lively English folk dance. During the summer months, you may have the opportunity to witness Morris dancers performing in the town.*

8. *Abingdon Michaelmas Fair: Held annually in October, the Abingdon Michaelmas Fair is one of the oldest and largest street fairs in the country. It features*

thrilling rides, games, food stalls, and a festive atmosphere.

Abingdon-on-Thames offers a delightful blend of history, riverside charm, and cultural experiences. Whether you're exploring its historic streets, visiting the remains of the abbey, or enjoying the riverside ambiance, Abingdon provides a rewarding destination for visitors interested in Oxfordshire's heritage.

WITNEY

Witney is a vibrant market town located in Oxfordshire, England. Situated on the River Windrush, it is known for its rich history, traditional architecture, and thriving market.

Location and Setting:

1. *Location: Witney is located approximately 12 miles (19 kilometers) west of Oxford. It is situated in the beautiful Oxfordshire countryside, surrounded by rolling hills and picturesque landscapes.*

Town Features:

2. *Market Square: The Market Square is the heart of Witney and is the focal point of the town's market, which has been held since the Middle Ages. The market takes place on various days of the week and offers a wide range of products, including fresh produce, crafts, clothing, and more.*

275

3. *St. Mary's Church: St. Mary's Church is a prominent landmark in Witney. Dating back to the 12th century, it features a striking tower and beautiful stained glass windows. The church is open to visitors and provides a glimpse into the town's history and architectural heritage.*

4. *Witney Blanket Industry: Witney has a significant historical association with the blanket industry. At its peak, Witney was renowned for producing high-quality blankets that were exported worldwide. Although the industry has declined, you can still learn about its history at the Witney and District Museum.*

276

5. *Traditional Architecture:* Witney showcases a mix of architectural styles, including timber-framed buildings, Georgian townhouses, and charming cottages. The town's streets are lined with independent shops, cafes, and pubs, creating a welcoming and characterful atmosphere.

6. *Cogges Manor Farm:* Located on the outskirts of Witney, Cogges Manor Farm is a historic working farm that offers a glimpse into rural life. Visitors can explore the farm's beautiful grounds, interact with farm animals, and learn about traditional farming practices.

Events and Festivals:

7. *Witney Feast: Witney Feast is an annual fair held in the town during September. It features exciting rides, games, food stalls, and entertainment for all ages. The fair has a long-standing tradition dating back to the 13th century.*

8. *Witney Carnival: The Witney Carnival is a colorful procession that takes place each July. It involves floats, costumes, music, and community participation, creating a festive atmosphere in the town.*

Witney's rich history, traditional architecture, and lively market make it an appealing destination in Oxfordshire. Whether you're exploring the Market Square, learning about the town's blanket industry, or enjoying the local events and festivals, Witney offers a delightful blend of heritage and community spirit.

BICESTER VILLAGE SHOPPING OUTLET

Bicester Village Shopping Outlet is a popular luxury shopping destination located in Bicester, Oxfordshire, England. It is part of the Bicester Village Shopping Collection, which includes several similar outlet villages around the world.

Location and Setting:

1. *Location: Bicester Village is situated in the town of Bicester, about 12 miles (19 kilometers) northeast of Oxford. It is*

conveniently located near major transportation routes and is easily accessible by car, train, or bus.

2. *Design and Layout: Bicester Village is designed as an open-air shopping village, resembling a traditional English village with pedestrianized streets. The architecture and landscaping create a pleasant and relaxed shopping environment.*

Shopping Experience:

3. *Luxury Brands: Bicester Village is known for its extensive collection of luxury and designer brands. It features more than 160 boutiques, offering a wide range*

281

of fashion, accessories, home goods, and more. Some of the well-known brands include Burberry, Gucci, Prada, Alexander McQueen, Jimmy Choo, and many others. The village offers discounted prices on previous seasons' collections, making it a favorite destination for fashion enthusiasts seeking designer bargains.

4. Boutique Shopping: The boutiques at Bicester Village are designed to resemble small, elegant storefronts. They provide a unique and intimate shopping experience with personalized service. The village is known for its attentive staff and curated selection of high-end products.

5. Dining and Cafés: Bicester Village offers a variety of dining options to cater to different tastes and preferences. You'll find cafes, restaurants, and food kiosks serving a range of cuisines, from casual snacks to fine dining experiences.

6. Services and Amenities: Bicester Village provides additional services and amenities to enhance the shopping experience. These may include personal shopping services, tax refund facilities for international visitors, luggage storage, and complimentary Wi-Fi.

Visitor Information:

7. *Opening Hours: Bicester Village is generally open seven days a week, including weekends and holidays. Opening hours may vary, so it's recommended to check the official website for the most up-to-date information.*

8. *Travel and Accessibility: Bicester Village is well-connected and easily accessible. It has its own train station, Bicester Village Station, which is served by direct trains from London and other major cities. The village also offers ample parking facilities for those arriving by car.*

Bicester Village Shopping Outlet is renowned for its luxury shopping experience, offering a wide range of designer brands in a charming village setting. Whether you're looking for fashion, accessories, or home goods, Bicester Village provides an opportunity to shop for high-end products at discounted prices.

285

THAME

Thame is a historic market town located in Oxfordshire, England. Situated about 13 miles (21 kilometers) east of Oxford, it is known for its charming streets, medieval architecture, and vibrant community.

Location and Setting:

1. *Location: Thame is located in the picturesque countryside of Oxfordshire. It is surrounded by rolling hills, farmland, and the River Thame, which gives the town its name.*

Town Features:

2. *Historic High Street: Thame's High Street is a focal point of the town and showcases its historic*

charm. The street is lined with traditional buildings, independent shops, cafes, and pubs. It offers a pleasant atmosphere for strolling, shopping, and soaking in the town's character.

3. Thame Museum: The Thame Museum is housed in a historic building and provides insights into the town's rich history. It features exhibits on local industries, notable figures, and the development of Thame over the centuries.

4. St. Mary's Church: St. Mary's Church is a prominent landmark in Thame, dating back to the 13th century. It features stunning

architecture, including a beautiful tower and intricate stained glass windows. The church is open to visitors and offers a glimpse into the town's religious heritage.

5. *Lord Williams's School: Founded in 1559, Lord Williams's School is a notable educational institution in Thame. The school's buildings add to the town's historic character and architectural appeal.*

6. *Thame Market: Thame has a long-standing tradition of holding markets, which continues to this day. The weekly market takes place on Tuesdays and offers a variety of goods, including fresh*

produce, crafts, clothing, and more.

Events and Festivals:

7. *Thame Fair: The Thame Fair is an annual event held in September. It features thrilling rides, games, food stalls, and entertainment, attracting both locals and visitors.*

8. *Thame Food Festival: The Thame Food Festival is a celebration of local and artisan food and drink. Held annually, it showcases a wide range of vendors, demonstrations, tastings, and other food-related activities.*

Thame's blend of history, traditional architecture, and community spirit make it a charming destination in Oxfordshire. Whether you're exploring the historic streets, visiting the local landmarks, or immersing yourself in the town's vibrant events, Thame provides a quintessential English market town experience.

CULINARY DELIGHTS

Oxfordshire is a haven for food enthusiasts, offering a delectable array of culinary delights that celebrate the region's diverse gastronomic heritage. From charming country pubs serving hearty traditional fare to stylish restaurants showcasing innovative cuisine, there is something to tantalize every palate in this vibrant county.

The county's rich agricultural landscape ensures an abundant supply of fresh, locally sourced ingredients, which are skillfully transformed into mouthwatering dishes that reflect both tradition and modernity.

Visitors can sample traditional Oxfordshire delicacies such as the famous Oxford Blue cheese, artisanal breads, and locally brewed ales. In addition, the region's fertile farmland yields an array of fresh produce, including succulent fruits, crisp vegetables, and tender meats, which form the cornerstone of many delightful dishes.

For those seeking a taste of luxury, Oxfordshire is home to several fine dining establishments that showcase the talents of acclaimed chefs, who artfully combine local and seasonal ingredients to create exquisite, Michelin-starred cuisine.

Beyond restaurants, the county's vibrant food scene extends to bustling farmers' markets, food festivals, and artisanal producers, where visitors can indulge in a treasure trove of gourmet delights, from artisan cheeses and handcrafted chocolates to organic fruit preserves and freshly baked pastries.

With its rich tapestry of culinary experiences, Oxfordshire invites visitors to embark on a gastronomic journey that celebrates the county's heritage, creativity, and passion for exceptional food and drink.

TRADITIONAL OXFORDSHIRE CUISINE

Traditional Oxfordshire cuisine reflects the agricultural heritage and local produce of the region. Here are some examples of traditional dishes and ingredients you might find in Oxfordshire:

1. *Oxford Sausages: Oxfordshire is known for its distinctive sausages, often referred to as Oxford sausages. They are typically made from a combination of pork, veal, breadcrumbs, and herbs, such as sage and thyme. These sausages have a unique flavor and are often enjoyed as part of a hearty breakfast or in traditional English dishes like bangers and mash.*

2. *Lamb and Beef: Oxfordshire's rural landscape lends itself to sheep and cattle farming, making lamb and beef popular meats in the region. Roast lamb with mint sauce and beef dishes like steak and ale pie or beef and vegetable stew are classic examples of Oxfordshire cuisine.*

3. *Game: Oxfordshire's countryside is home to an abundance of game, including pheasant, partridge, and venison. These meats are often featured in traditional dishes, such as game pies or roasted game birds served with seasonal vegetables.*

4. *Oxford Blue Cheese: Oxfordshire is known for its production of Oxford Blue cheese, which is a creamy and tangy blue cheese with a distinct flavor. It's made from locally sourced cow's milk and is often enjoyed on cheeseboards or crumbled into salads.*

5. *Apple Recipes: Oxfordshire has a long history of apple orchards, and apples are a prominent ingredient in traditional Oxfordshire cuisine. Apple pies, apple crumbles, and apple sauces are popular desserts and can be paired with locally produced cream or custard.*

6. *Cotswold Butter: The Cotswolds, an area that stretches into Oxfordshire, is renowned for its high-quality dairy products. Cotswold butter, made from the rich milk of the region, is known for its creamy texture and rich flavor. It is often used in baking and cooking.*

7. *Ploughman's Lunch: While not unique to Oxfordshire, the Ploughman's Lunch is a classic British dish that is often enjoyed in the region. It typically consists of a selection of local cheeses, pickles, cold meats, crusty bread, and a side of salad, creating a satisfying and hearty meal.*

These are just a few examples of traditional Oxfordshire cuisine. The region's agricultural heritage and access to local ingredients contribute to a rich culinary tradition that celebrates local produce and flavors.

LOCAL FOOD MARKET

Oxfordshire is home to several vibrant food markets where you can find a variety of locally produced goods. Here are some popular food markets in Oxfordshire:

1. *Oxford Covered Market (Oxford): Located in the heart of Oxford, the Covered Market is a historic indoor market that has been operating for over 200 years. It is home to numerous food stalls offering fresh produce, meats, cheeses, baked goods, and more. You can find a range of local products and specialty items, as well as international cuisine.*

2. *Witney Market (Witney): Witney holds a weekly market on*

Thursdays and Saturdays in the town center, where you can find a variety of goods, including fresh produce, meats, baked goods, and plants. The market also features artisanal products and crafts from local vendors.

3. *Thame Farmers' Market (Thame): The Thame Farmers' Market takes place on the second Tuesday of every month and showcases a range of locally produced goods. You can find fresh fruits and vegetables, meats, cheeses, bread, pastries, honey, jams, and more. It's a great opportunity to support local farmers and artisans.*

4. *Banbury Market (Banbury): Banbury's general market, held on Thursdays and Saturdays, includes food stalls where you can find fresh produce, meats, cheeses, baked goods, and other local products. The market also offers a variety of non-food items, making it a bustling and diverse shopping experience.*

5. *Henley-on-Thames Farmers' Market (Henley-on-Thames): The Henley-on-Thames Farmers' Market takes place on the fourth Thursday of every month. It features a selection of local producers offering fresh fruits and vegetables, meats, cheeses, bread, pastries, and more. It's a*

great opportunity to discover the region's culinary delights.

6. *Wallingford Local Producers' Market (Wallingford): The Wallingford Local Producers' Market is held on the third Saturday of each month. It brings together local farmers, bakers, and producers who offer a wide range of fresh produce, meats, cheeses, bread, cakes, honey, and other artisanal products.*

These are just a few examples of the many food markets in Oxfordshire. Visiting these markets allows you to support local producers, discover fresh and seasonal ingredients, and

experience the vibrant culinary scene
of the region.

PUBS AND RESTAURANT

Oxfordshire offers a diverse range of pubs and restaurants, catering to various tastes and preferences. Whether you're looking for traditional British cuisine, international flavors, or fine dining experiences, there are plenty of options to explore. Here are some notable pubs and restaurants in Oxfordshire:

Pubs:

1. *The Trout Inn (Wolvercote, Oxford): Located on the banks of the River Thames, The Trout Inn is a historic pub known for its picturesque setting and traditional British pub fare. It offers a cozy atmosphere and a riverside terrace for outdoor dining.*

2. The Perch (Binsey, Oxford): The Perch is another charming riverside pub, known for its beautiful gardens and outdoor seating. It serves a mix of classic British dishes and modern cuisine, focusing on locally sourced ingredients.

3. The King's Arms (Woodstock): Situated in the historic town of Woodstock, The King's Arms is a traditional pub with a warm and welcoming atmosphere. It offers a menu featuring British pub classics, along with a selection of real ales and wines.

4. *The Chequers Inn (Burcot, Abingdon): This 16th-century thatched inn offers a rustic ambiance and a menu of traditional pub food with a modern twist. It's known for its hearty meals, cask ales, and Sunday roasts.*

Restaurants:

1. *Le Manoir aux Quat'Saisons (Great Milton, Oxford): This renowned Michelin-starred restaurant, set in a stunning manor house, offers a world-class dining experience. It focuses on French cuisine with an emphasis on seasonal and locally sourced ingredients.*

2. *The Crazy Bear (Stadhampton): The Crazy Bear is a unique and stylish restaurant that combines Thai and English influences. It features opulent décor, an extensive cocktail menu, and a fusion of flavors in its dishes.*

3. *The Nut Tree (Murcott): The Nut Tree is a Michelin-starred gastropub known for its innovative and refined British cuisine. It offers a menu that showcases the best of local produce and has a relaxed and welcoming atmosphere.*

4. *The Old Parsonage Hotel (Oxford): The Old Parsonage Hotel houses a restaurant that*

*serves modern British cuisine
with a seasonal and locally
inspired menu. The elegant
setting and attentive service
make it a popular choice for
special occasions.*

These are just a few examples of the
many pubs and restaurants in
Oxfordshire. Whether you're seeking a
traditional pub experience or a fine
dining adventure, Oxfordshire's
culinary scene has something to satisfy
every palate.

AFTERNOON TEA EXPERIENCES

Oxfordshire offers several establishments where you can indulge in the quintessentially British tradition of afternoon tea. These are some notable places to enjoy afternoon tea experiences in Oxfordshire:

1. *The Randolph Hotel (Oxford):*
   The Randolph Hotel, located in the heart of Oxford, offers a traditional afternoon tea experience in a sophisticated setting. You can enjoy a selection of finger sandwiches, scones with clotted cream and jam, and an assortment of delicate pastries and cakes.

309

2. *The Manor at Weston-on-the-Green (Weston-on-the-Green): This luxury hotel and restaurant provides a delightful afternoon tea experience. Set in a historic manor house, it offers a range of teas, accompanied by freshly baked scones, finger sandwiches, and an array of sweet treats.*

3. *Blenheim Palace (Woodstock): Blenheim Palace, a UNESCO World Heritage Site, offers afternoon tea in its elegant Orangery restaurant. You can enjoy tea while overlooking the breathtaking palace grounds. The menu typically includes a selection of sandwiches, scones,*

pastries, and, of course, a choice
of teas.

4. The Crazy Bear (Stadhampton):
   The Crazy Bear, known for its
   unique and lavish décor, also
   offers an afternoon tea
   experience. You can expect an
   unconventional twist on the
   traditional tea, with an array of
   savory and sweet delights served
   in their distinctive setting.

5. The Feathers (Woodstock): The
   Feathers is a historic coaching
   inn in Woodstock that offers a
   delightful afternoon tea
   experience. You can relax in their
   cozy lounge or courtyard and
   enjoy a selection of finger

sandwiches, scones, and a
variety of cakes and pastries.

6. *The Old Parsonage Hotel*
   (Oxford): The Old Parsonage
   Hotel provides a charming
   setting for afternoon tea. You
   can savor a selection of
   sandwiches, warm scones, and
   an assortment of cakes and
   pastries, accompanied by your
   choice of tea or coffee.

Whether you prefer a traditional
experience in a historic setting or a
more contemporary twist on this
beloved tradition, these establishments
offer delightful options to indulge in a
leisurely afternoon tea experience.

BREWERIES AND WINERIES

Oxfordshire is home to a number of breweries and wineries where you can explore and sample a variety of locally crafted beers and wines. These are some notable breweries and wineries in Oxfordshire:

Breweries:

1. *Hook Norton Brewery (Hook Norton): Hook Norton Brewery is one of the oldest family-run breweries in England, dating back to 1849. Located in the picturesque village of Hook Norton, the brewery offers guided tours where you can learn about the brewing process and*

taste their range of traditional ales.

2. *White Horse Brewery (Stanford in the Vale): White Horse Brewery is an independent microbrewery known for its range of award-winning real ales. They produce a variety of styles, from classic bitters to hop-forward IPAs. They occasionally offer brewery tours and have an on-site shop where you can purchase their beers.*

3. *Loose Cannon Brewery (Abingdon): Loose Cannon Brewery is a craft brewery that specializes in creating innovative and flavorful beers. They*

produce a range of traditional and contemporary styles, including pale ales, IPAs, stouts, and seasonal brews. The brewery offers tours and tastings by appointment.

Wineries:

1. *Bothy Vineyard (Fringford): Bothy Vineyard is a family-run winery that produces a range of English wines, including still and sparkling varieties. They specialize in organic and biodynamic viticulture and offer tours and tastings where you can learn about their winemaking processes and sample their wines.*

2. Brightwell Vineyard (Wallingford): Brightwell Vineyard is situated on the slopes of the Chiltern Hills and produces a range of award-winning English wines. They offer vineyard tours, where you can explore the vineyard and learn about their winemaking techniques. Tastings of their wines are also available.

3. Wytham Vineyard (Oxford): Wytham Vineyard is a small-scale winery located just outside Oxford. They produce limited quantities of handcrafted wines, including white, rosé, and sparkling wines. The vineyard occasionally hosts open days and events where visitors can sample

their wines and learn about the winemaking process.

Exploring these establishments allows you to discover and appreciate the local craftsmanship and flavors in the region's beers and wines. It's always a good idea to check their websites or contact them directly for tour availability and opening hours.

FESTIVALS AND EVENTS

Oxfordshire is a vibrant county with a diverse array of festivals and events that cater to a wide range of interests. From cultural celebrations and music festivals to food fairs and traditional carnivals, there is always something exciting happening in this dynamic region.

The county plays host to an eclectic mix of music festivals, ranging from large-scale events featuring internationally renowned artists to smaller, more intimate gatherings that showcase emerging talents across various genres. Whether you're a fan of rock, folk, classical, or electronic music, you're sure to find a festival that will strike the right chord.

318

For those with a penchant for the arts, Oxfordshire offers a rich calendar of cultural events, including theatre productions, art exhibitions, and literary festivals that celebrate the county's creative spirit. Visitors can immerse themselves in the world of literature, visual arts, and performing arts, all within the captivating backdrop of Oxfordshire's picturesque landscapes and historic venues.

Foodies will delight in the array of food and drink festivals that take place throughout the year, featuring local artisanal producers, specialty vendors, and renowned chefs showcasing the region's culinary talents. From wine tastings and farmers' markets to gourmet food trails and street food extravaganzas, there's no shortage of epicurean experiences to indulge in.

Traditional events such as country fairs, agricultural shows, and historical reenactments offer a glimpse into Oxfordshire's rich heritage and provide fun-filled entertainment for the whole family. Whether it's cheering on participants in a classic car rally, marvelling at the displays of local craftsmanship, or enjoying the spectacle of historical pageantry, there's always something to captivate and entertain.

With its diverse and dynamic calendar of events, Oxfordshire is a county that pulsates with energy and offers visitors an abundance of opportunities to connect, celebrate, and immerse

themselves in the cultural tapestry of
the region.

OXFORD LITERARY FESTIVALS

Oxford is renowned for its rich literary heritage, and it hosts several literary festivals throughout the year. These festivals celebrate literature in its various forms, including author talks, panel discussions, book signings, and more.

1. *Oxford Literary Festival: The Oxford Literary Festival is one of the most prominent literary events in the city. Held annually in the spring, it brings together a diverse range of authors, poets, and speakers from around the world. The festival features a wide array of events, including lectures, debates, workshops, and readings, covering a broad*

range of literary genres and themes.

2. *Oxford Children's Literature Festival:* As the name suggests, the Oxford Children's Literature Festival focuses specifically on children's literature. It aims to inspire a love of reading among young audiences and features a lineup of renowned children's authors and illustrators. The festival includes storytelling sessions, workshops, performances, and interactive events designed to engage children and nurture their creative imagination.

3. *Oxford Translation Day: Oxford Translation Day is a literary festival that celebrates literary translation and its vital role in promoting global literary exchange. The festival showcases the work of translators and explores the art and craft of translation through panel discussions, workshops, and readings. It provides a platform for translators and authors to discuss their collaborative processes and the challenges and opportunities involved in translating literary works.*

4. *St Hilda's Crime and Mystery Weekend: Organized by St Hilda's College, University of Oxford, the Crime and Mystery*

Weekend is dedicated to the genre of crime fiction and mystery writing. The festival features talks, panel discussions, and workshops with crime writers, exploring various aspects of crime fiction, from classic detective novels to contemporary thrillers.

5. *Oxford Poetry Festival: The Oxford Poetry Festival celebrates the art of poetry through readings, performances, workshops, and discussions. It brings together established and emerging poets, providing a platform for them to share their work and engage with poetry enthusiasts. The festival often includes open mic sessions and*

opportunities for aspiring poets to showcase their talent.

Each festival offers a unique experience and provides an opportunity to engage with literature, authors, and the vibrant literary community in the city. It's worth checking the official websites of these festivals for the latest information on dates, schedules, and ticketing.

COWLEY ROAD CARNIVAL

The Cowley Road Carnival is an annual multicultural street festival that takes place in Oxford, specifically on Cowley Road. It is one of the largest and most vibrant community events in the city, attracting thousands of people each year. The carnival celebrates the diverse cultures, music, food, and arts of the local community. The Cowley Road Carnival features a lively procession of colorful floats, dancers, musicians, and performers parading along Cowley Road. Participants showcase their cultural heritage through costumes, music, and dance, representing various countries and traditions. The procession creates a festive and vibrant atmosphere, with spectators lining the streets to cheer and enjoy the spectacle. In addition to the procession, the carnival offers a range of activities and entertainment for people of all ages. There are multiple stages featuring live music performances from local bands and artists, showcasing a variety of musical genres. You can also find food stalls serving delicious international cuisine, craft stalls selling handmade products, and various interactive activities for children. The Cowley Road Carnival typically takes place in the summer months, usually in July. It is organized by a team of volunteers and supported by local businesses, community groups, and organizations. The carnival is a fantastic opportunity to experience the multicultural spirit of Oxford, enjoy live music, indulge in diverse food, and celebrate the vibrant community that resides along Cowley Road. It's worth noting that event details, dates, and specific activities may vary from year to year, so it is advisable to check the official Cowley Road Carnival website or local event listings for the most up-to-date information if you plan to attend.

HENLEY ROYAL REGATTA

The Henley Royal Regatta is one of the most prestigious and renowned rowing events in the world. It takes place annually on the River Thames in Henley-on-Thames, Oxfordshire, England. The regatta attracts elite rowers from around the globe and offers a thrilling showcase of competitive rowing.

The regatta is steeped in tradition and history, dating back to its founding in 1839. It spans over five days, usually starting on the first Wednesday in July. The event draws a large crowd, including rowing enthusiasts, spectators, and social attendees.

The Henley Royal Regatta features a series of rowing races, primarily in the

330

form of side-by-side knock-out competitions. The races take place along a 2,112-meter (1.31-mile) stretch of the River Thames, known as the Henley Reach. Competing crews race in various boat classes, including eights, fours, pairs, and single sculls.

Spectators can enjoy the races from various vantage points, including the Stewards' Enclosure, where ticket holders can access exclusive areas with excellent views of the course. There are also grandstands, riverside enclosures, and public areas along the riverbank where people can watch the races. The regatta offers a festive atmosphere, with food stalls, bars, and entertainment options available for visitors.

In addition to the rowing competitions, the Henley Royal Regatta has a social aspect. It is an opportunity for attendees to dress in formal attire, including blazers and dresses, and enjoy socializing and networking in a unique setting. The regatta is known for its strict dress code and maintains a sense of elegance and tradition throughout the event.

Attending the Henley Royal Regatta provides a fantastic opportunity to witness world-class rowing, soak up the lively atmosphere, and experience the rich heritage of this historic sporting event. It is advisable to check the official Henley Royal Regatta website for specific dates, ticket information, and any updates or changes to the event schedule.

BLENHEIM PALACE FLOWER SHOW

The Blenheim Palace Flower Show is a delightful horticultural event that takes place in the stunning setting of Blenheim Palace, a UNESCO World Heritage site located in Oxfordshire, England. The show features a spectacular display of flowers, plants, and gardens, offering visitors an

333

opportunity to immerse themselves in the beauty and diversity of the natural world.

Throughout the show, attendees can explore an array of carefully curated floral exhibits, showcasing innovative garden designs, rare botanical specimens, and vibrant floral arrangements. From traditional English gardens to contemporary landscape designs, the show provides inspiration for gardening enthusiasts and nature lovers alike.

In addition to the stunning floral displays, the Blenheim Palace Flower Show offers a wealth of activities and attractions to engage visitors of all ages. Horticultural enthusiasts can partake in gardening demonstrations, workshops, and lectures presented by experts, providing valuable insights and practical tips for cultivating their own green spaces.

The event also features a marketplace where attendees can peruse a diverse selection of gardening supplies, plants, and artisanal products, offering the perfect opportunity to source unique additions for their own gardens or outdoor spaces.

Beyond the floral festivities, the Blenheim Palace Flower Show provides a captivating backdrop for leisurely strolls, picnics, and outdoor enjoyment amidst the palace's picturesque grounds. Visitors can revel in the splendor of the historic landscape, taking in the breathtaking architecture,

335

manicured lawns, and serene water features that make Blenheim Palace a quintessential English country estate.

The Blenheim Palace Flower Show is a celebration of nature's beauty and a testament to the artistry and skill of horticultural enthusiasts and garden designers. Whether you're a green-fingered gardening aficionado or simply appreciate the wonders of the natural world, the show offers a memorable experience that is sure to both inspire and enchant.

CHRISTMAS MARKETS AND FESTIVALS

Oxfordshire and its surrounding areas host several Christmas markets and festivals during the holiday season. These events offer a festive atmosphere, unique shopping opportunities, delicious food and drink, and entertainment.

1. *Oxford Christmas Market: The Oxford Christmas Market takes place in the heart of Oxford, usually in the historic setting of Broad Street. The market features over 50 stalls selling a variety of gifts, crafts, decorations, and food. Visitors can enjoy live music, festive performances, and indulge in seasonal treats.*

337

2. *Blenheim Palace Christmas Market: Blenheim Palace, located in Woodstock, hosts a Christmas market on its grounds. The market offers a range of stalls selling gifts, crafts, food, and drinks. Visitors can also explore the beautifully decorated palace and enjoy festive activities and entertainment.*

3. *Thame Country Fair Christmas Shopping Fayre: The Thame Country Fair Christmas Shopping Fayre is held at Thame Showground, just outside Oxfordshire. The fair features a wide variety of stalls selling unique gifts, artisan products, and festive decorations. There*

are also demonstrations, live entertainment, and food and drink options.

4. *Bicester Christmas Market: Bicester, a town in Oxfordshire, hosts a Christmas market with a mix of stalls selling crafts, gifts, and food. The market often includes live entertainment, carol singing, and family-friendly activities.*

5. *Henley-on-Thames Christmas Festival: Henley-on-Thames, located on the River Thames, hosts a Christmas festival with a range of activities. The festival includes a traditional Christmas market, live music performances,*

*street entertainment, and a
lantern procession.*

It's worth noting that event details and dates may vary from year to year, so it's recommended to check the official websites or local event listings for the most up-to-date information about specific markets and festivals you are interested in attending.

FAMILY-FRIENDLY ACTIVITIES

Oxfordshire offers a wide range of family-friendly activities, making it an ideal destination for fun and memorable experiences for visitors of all ages. From exploring historic sites to enjoying outdoor adventures, the county provides a diverse array of attractions that cater to families seeking entertainment and quality time together.

One of the most iconic family-friendly attractions in Oxfordshire is the Cotswold Wildlife Park and Gardens, where visitors can encounter a fascinating menagerie of animals from around the world. The park's spacious grounds and beautifully landscaped gardens offer the perfect setting for a leisurely stroll while observing exotic wildlife, making it an educational and entertaining day out for families.

For a blend of history and adventure, families can explore the enchanting Blenheim Palace, a UNESCO World Heritage site set amidst breathtaking parkland. The palace offers a range of

341

family-friendly activities, including interactive tours, outdoor trails, and seasonal events, providing an immersive experience that showcases both the grandeur of the estate and its rich heritage.

Additionally, Oxfordshire is home to an array of picturesque parks and nature reserves that are perfect for outdoor recreation and exploration. Families can embark on leisurely walks, picnics, and wildlife spotting in locations such as Shotover Country Park, Buscot Park, or the Oxford University Parks, providing an opportunity to enjoy the county's natural beauty and tranquility.

Furthermore, the county's vibrant market towns and villages offer a wealth of family-oriented attractions, including interactive museums, farm parks, and charming riverside promenades that create an inviting atmosphere for leisurely family outings.

With its diverse range of family-friendly activities, Oxfordshire presents ample opportunities for creating cherished memories and enjoying quality time together amidst the county's rich history and natural splendor. Whether exploring wildlife parks, historic estates, or scenic outdoor spaces, families are sure to find an abundance of engaging and enjoyable experiences throughout Oxfordshire.

COTSWOLDS WILDLIFE PARK AND GARDENS

The Cotswolds Wildlife Park and Gardens is a popular attraction located in Burford, Oxfordshire, within the picturesque Cotswolds region. It is a zoological park that offers visitors the opportunity to see a wide variety of animals and explore beautifully landscaped gardens. Some information about the park:

Animal Exhibits: The wildlife park is home to over 260 different species of animals from around the world. Visitors can see animals such as lions, giraffes, rhinos, zebras, meerkats, penguins, lemurs, reptiles, birds, and many more. The park focuses on conservation and provides a natural and spacious environment for the animals.

Gardens: In addition to the animal exhibits, the Cotswolds Wildlife Park features stunning gardens spread across 160 acres of parkland. The gardens showcase a diverse range of plants, including exotic and rare species. Visitors can stroll through the walled garden, the tropical house, the prairie garden, and the stunning rhododendron walk.

Interactive Experiences: The park offers various interactive experiences and activities that allow visitors to get closer to the animals. These may include feeding sessions, talks by the park's knowledgeable staff, and encounters with some of the park's friendlier residents.

Children's Farmyard: The Cotswolds Wildlife Park has a dedicated Children's Farmyard where younger visitors can interact with domesticated animals such as goats, sheep, chickens, rabbits, and guinea pigs. They can also enjoy tractor rides and play areas.

Conservation and Education: The park is committed to conservation efforts and participates in breeding programs for endangered species. It also provides educational programs and resources to raise awareness about wildlife conservation and the importance of protecting natural habitats.

Refreshments and Facilities: The park has a café and picnic areas where visitors can enjoy refreshments and meals. There is also a gift shop where you can find souvenirs and animal-themed merchandise.

The Cotswolds Wildlife Park and Gardens offers a memorable experience for animal lovers, nature enthusiasts, and families. It provides an opportunity to observe a wide range of animals, explore beautiful gardens, and learn about wildlife conservation. It's advisable to check the park's website for the most up-to-date information on opening times, admission prices, special events, and any COVID-19 safety measures that may be in place.

CROCODILES OF THE
WORLD

348

"Crocodiles of the World" is a crocodile conservation and education center located in Brize Norton, Oxfordshire, United Kingdom. It is the UK's only crocodile zoo and is dedicated to the conservation of crocodiles and their habitats.

Exhibits: The center houses a wide variety of crocodiles and alligators from different parts of the world. Visitors can see various species, including Nile crocodiles, American alligators, Cuban crocodiles, spectacled caimans, and more. The exhibits provide an opportunity to observe these fascinating reptiles up close and learn about their biology, behavior, and conservation.

Conservation and Research: Crocodiles of the World actively supports conservation efforts for crocodiles and their habitats. The center collaborates with other organizations and conducts research to contribute to the understanding and conservation of these species. They also provide expertise and resources for crocodile conservation projects around the world.

Education and Outreach: The center aims to raise awareness and educate the public about crocodiles and their ecological importance. They offer educational programs, talks, and guided tours to educate visitors about crocodile biology, conservation challenges, and the need to protect their habitats.

Experiences and Activities: Crocodiles of the World provides various interactive experiences for visitors. These include "Meet the Crocs" sessions where visitors can get up close to some of the smaller crocodiles and learn more about them from the expert staff. The center also offers crocodile feeding demonstrations and opportunities for visitors to handle certain reptiles under supervision.

Facilities: The center has facilities such as a café, picnic area, and a gift shop where visitors can purchase souvenirs and educational materials related to crocodiles.

Crocodiles of the World provides an opportunity to learn about these fascinating creatures and the conservation challenges they face. It offers an engaging and educational experience for visitors of all ages. It's recommended to check the center's website for the most up-to-date information on opening hours, ticket prices, special events, and any COVID-19 safety protocols that may be in place.

CUTTESLOWE PARK

Cutteslowe Park is a public park located in the Cutteslowe and Sunnymead area of Oxford, England. It is a popular recreational space that offers a range of amenities and activities for visitors of all ages.

Park Features: Cutteslowe Park covers a large area and features expansive green spaces, well-maintained gardens, and a variety of recreational facilities. The park offers playgrounds for children, including climbing frames, swings, and slides. There are also sports fields, tennis courts, and a skate park for those looking to engage in outdoor activities.

Miniature Railway: One of the highlights of Cutteslowe Park is the miniature railway, known as the North Oxfordshire Model Engineering Society (NOME) Railway. It operates on select days and provides rides for children and adults alike, offering a fun and nostalgic experience.

Ponds and Wildlife: The park includes several ponds, which are home to a variety of wildlife. Visitors can enjoy observing ducks, swans, and other bird species that inhabit the ponds. The park's natural areas and woodland also attract a range of wildlife.

Café and Refreshments: Cutteslowe Park has a café where visitors can purchase refreshments, snacks, and light meals. It provides a pleasant spot to take a break and enjoy a drink or a bite to eat.

Events and Festivals: Throughout the year, Cutteslowe Park hosts various events and festivals. These may include community gatherings, music concerts, fairs, and seasonal celebrations. It's worth checking the park's website or local event listings to see if any events are scheduled during your visit.

Walking and Cycling Paths: The park offers paved paths that are ideal for leisurely walks, jogging, or cycling. The paths wind through the park, providing opportunities to explore its different areas and enjoy the natural surroundings.

Cutteslowe Park is a lovely green space that offers a range of activities and

355

amenities for individuals, families, and friends to enjoy. Whether you're looking for a peaceful stroll, a place to play sports, or a spot to relax and have a picnic, Cutteslowe Park provides a welcoming environment.

MILLETS FARM CENTRE

Millets Farm Centre is a family-friendly attraction located in Frilford, near Abingdon, Oxfordshire, United Kingdom. It offers a range of activities, shopping opportunities, and dining options.

Farm Shop: Millets Farm Centre is known for its large farm shop, which offers a wide variety of fresh produce, including fruits, vegetables, dairy products, meats, and baked goods. Visitors can purchase locally sourced and seasonal items, as well as specialty products.

Pick Your Own: One of the main attractions at Millets Farm Centre is their "Pick Your Own" fields. Depending on the season, visitors can pick strawberries, raspberries, blackberries, apples, pumpkins, and other fruits and vegetables. It provides a fun and interactive experience for individuals and families.

Animal Walkway: The centre features an animal walkway where visitors can see and interact with various farm animals. There are opportunities to feed and pet animals such as goats, rabbits, guinea pigs, and more. It's a great way for children to learn about farm animals up close.

Maize Maze: During the summer months, Millets Farm Centre creates a Maize Maze, offering visitors a fun and challenging activity. The maze is themed each year, with puzzles and clues to navigate through the towering cornfield.

Play Area and Falconry Centre: The centre has a large outdoor play area with slides, climbing frames, and other attractions for children. Additionally, there is a Falconry Centre where visitors can learn about birds of prey and watch flying displays.

Cafés and Restaurants: Millets Farm Centre has several dining options, including a café, a tearoom, and a restaurant. Visitors can enjoy a range of meals, snacks, and beverages, often featuring locally sourced ingredients.

Shopping and Events: The centre hosts various events throughout the year, including seasonal celebrations, craft fairs, and food festivals. There are also shops selling garden supplies, home décor, gifts, toys, and more.

Millets Farm Centre offers a diverse range of activities and experiences for visitors of all ages. It's advisable to check their website or contact them directly for the most up-to-date information on opening hours, specific attractions, seasonal availability, and any special events or activities that may be happening during your visit.

WATERPERRY GARDENS

Waterperry Gardens is a beautiful and historic garden located in Waterperry village, near Wheatley, Oxfordshire, United Kingdom. It is known for its stunning horticultural displays, tranquil atmosphere, and rich history.

Garden Features: Waterperry Gardens cover eight acres and feature a variety of gardens, each with its own unique theme and planting style. Visitors can explore the formal gardens, including the herbaceous border, the rose garden, the lily canal, and the classical pool. There are also tranquil water gardens, a riverside walk, and a beautiful orchard.

Herbaceous Border: One of the highlights of Waterperry Gardens is its

361

famous herbaceous border, which stretches for 200 meters. It is filled with a vibrant display of colorful flowers and plants, creating a stunning visual impact.

Tea Shop and Restaurant: Waterperry Gardens has a tea shop and a restaurant where visitors can enjoy refreshments and meals. They serve a selection of homemade cakes, light lunches, afternoon teas, and other delicious treats. The tea shop often uses ingredients sourced from the gardens, providing a farm-to-table experience.

Plant Centre: The gardens have a plant centre where visitors can purchase a wide range of plants, including perennials, shrubs, climbers, and herbs. The centre offers knowledgeable staff who can provide advice and guidance on plant selection and care.

Art and Craft Gallery: Waterperry Gardens also houses an art and craft gallery, showcasing the work of local artists and craftspeople. Visitors can browse and purchase a variety of unique and handmade items, including ceramics, paintings, textiles, and jewelry.

Courses and Workshops: The gardens offer a range of horticultural courses and workshops throughout the year. These sessions cover various topics such as gardening techniques, plant care, flower arranging, and more. It's an opportunity for visitors to learn new skills and deepen their knowledge of gardening.

Events: Waterperry Gardens hosts seasonal events and festivals, including garden fairs, plant sales, art exhibitions, and Christmas markets. These events provide additional opportunities for visitors to explore the gardens and enjoy a range of activities and entertainment.

Waterperry Gardens is a delightful destination for garden enthusiasts, nature lovers, and those seeking a peaceful and picturesque setting. It's recommended to check their website for the most up-to-date information on opening hours, admission fees, special events, and any specific guidelines or restrictions that may be in place.

OXFORD ICE RINK

The Oxford Ice Rink is a popular ice skating facility located in Oxford, England. It offers a range of ice skating activities for individuals, families, and groups.

Ice Skating Sessions: The rink provides various public skating sessions throughout the week, allowing visitors of all ages and skill levels to enjoy ice skating. These sessions typically include general skating, family sessions, and disco skating with music and lighting effects.

Ice Hockey: The Oxford Ice Rink is also home to ice hockey teams and offers ice hockey training and matches. Ice hockey enthusiasts can participate in training sessions or watch exciting ice hockey games.

Figure Skating: The rink provides opportunities for figure skaters to practice and develop their skills. There may be dedicated sessions for figure skating practice, as well as coaching available for skaters looking to improve their technique.

Skate Hire: For those who don't have their own ice skates, the rink offers skate hire services. Visitors can rent ice skates in various sizes, ensuring that everyone can participate in the skating sessions.

Ice Skating Lessons: The rink offers ice skating lessons for beginners and

367

those looking to improve their skating abilities. These lessons are typically provided by qualified instructors who can guide skaters through the basics or help them refine their techniques.

Parties and Events: The Oxford Ice Rink also caters to private parties, birthdays, and group events. They offer packages that include exclusive use of the ice rink and additional services such as party rooms and catering.

Facilities: The rink provides amenities such as changing rooms, lockers, and a café where visitors can grab refreshments and snacks.

It's important to note that the availability of specific sessions, lessons, and events may vary, so it's advisable to check the Oxford Ice Rink's website or contact them directly for the most up-to-date information on opening times, admission fees, skate hire, lessons, and any special events or promotions they may have.

DAY TRIPS FROM OXFORDSHIRE

Oxfordshire's central location in the heart of England makes it an excellent starting point for a variety of exciting day trips to explore the surrounding regions. Whether you're interested in historic landmarks, natural attractions, or charming towns, there are numerous options within easy reach of Oxfordshire that offer diverse experiences for day-trippers.

For travelers seeking a cultural and historical journey, a day trip to Stratford-upon-Avon, the birthplace of William Shakespeare, provides an immersive exploration of the renowned playwright's life and legacy. Visitors can tour Shakespeare's birthplace, visit the Royal Shakespeare Theatre, and meander through the picturesque streets of this charming market town, offering a blend of history, culture, and scenic beauty.

Alternatively, for those with a penchant for stunning landscapes and outdoor adventures, the Cotswolds, an Area of Outstanding Natural Beauty, is a perfect destination for a day trip from Oxfordshire. With its quaint villages, rolling hills, and scenic walking paths, the Cotswolds offer a quintessentially English countryside experience, inviting visitors to soak in the serene beauty and idyllic charm of the region.

History enthusiasts and architecture aficionados may find a day trip to the city of Bath particularly captivating.

Renowned for its well-preserved Roman baths, splendid Georgian architecture, and rich cultural heritage, Bath provides a remarkable blend of history, culture, and relaxation, making it a rewarding day trip destination for visitors of all interests.

For those with a fascination for grand stately homes and beautiful gardens, a day trip to the majestic Chatsworth House in Derbyshire offers a captivating glimpse into the opulent lifestyle of the aristocracy. Set amidst breathtaking landscapes, Chatsworth House boasts an array of art collections, ornate furnishings, and meticulously landscaped gardens, providing a feast for the senses and a memorable day out for visitors.

Additionally, the city of London, with its iconic landmarks, world-class museums, and vibrant atmosphere, is within easy reach for a day trip from Oxfordshire. Whether exploring the British Museum, taking a stroll along the Thames, or visiting the Tower of London, a day in the UK's capital city promises an exciting blend of history, culture, and entertainment.

With its convenient location, Oxfordshire serves as an ideal launchpad for day trips to an array of captivating destinations, offering something for everyone, from history buffs and nature lovers to urban explorers and cultural enthusiasts. Whether seeking a tranquil retreat in the countryside or an action-packed day in the city, the surrounding regions provide an array of options to cater to diverse interests and create memorable experiences for day-trippers from Oxfordshire.

STRATFORD-UPON-AVON

Stratford-upon-Avon is a historic market town located in Warwickshire, England. It is famous worldwide as the birthplace of the renowned playwright William Shakespeare.

Shakespeare's Birthplace: One of the main attractions in Stratford-upon-Avon is Shakespeare's Birthplace, a restored 16th-century half-timbered house where William Shakespeare was born and spent his early years. Visitors can explore the house, see exhibitions about Shakespeare's life and works, and gain insights into the playwright's early influences.

Royal Shakespeare Theatre: The Royal Shakespeare Theatre is a world-renowned theater located in Stratford-upon-Avon. It hosts a variety of productions, including Shakespearean plays, contemporary dramas, and musicals. The theater offers an opportunity to experience high-quality performances in a historic and iconic setting.

Shakespeare's Family Homes: Aside from Shakespeare's Birthplace, Stratford-upon-Avon is home to several other properties associated with Shakespeare and his family. These include Anne Hathaway's Cottage (the childhood home of Shakespeare's wife), Mary Arden's Farm (the childhood home of Shakespeare's mother), Hall's Croft (the home of Shakespeare's daughter and her husband), and New Place (the site of Shakespeare's final residence).

Holy Trinity Church: Holy Trinity Church is a beautiful medieval church situated on the banks of the River Avon. It is the final resting place of William Shakespeare and is open to visitors. The church's stunning architecture and historical significance make it a must-visit attraction in Stratford-upon-Avon.

River Avon: The River Avon flows through the town, adding to its scenic charm. Visitors can take a boat trip along the river, hire a rowing boat, or simply enjoy a leisurely stroll along its picturesque banks.

Stratford-upon-Avon Canal: The town is also connected to the Stratford-upon-Avon Canal, which offers opportunities for walking, cycling, and boating. The canal provides a tranquil setting and beautiful views of the surrounding countryside.

Town Center and Shopping: Stratford-upon-Avon's town center is filled with charming streets, Tudor-style buildings, independent shops, boutiques, and restaurants. It's a delightful place to explore, shop for unique souvenirs, and enjoy a meal or a traditional afternoon tea.

Stratford-upon-Avon offers a rich cultural experience, allowing visitors to immerse themselves in the life and works of William Shakespeare. With its historic landmarks, theaters, natural beauty, and vibrant town center, it attracts tourists from around the world.

379

BATH

Bath is a historic city located in Somerset, England, known for its Roman-built baths, stunning Georgian architecture, and rich cultural heritage.

Roman Baths: The Roman Baths are one of the most iconic attractions in Bath. These ancient thermal baths date back to Roman times and are remarkably well-preserved. Visitors can explore the baths, learn about their history, and view the fascinating artifacts on display.

Bath Abbey: Bath Abbey is a magnificent medieval church with striking Gothic architecture. It is located in the heart of the city and is known for its intricate stonework, stained glass windows, and beautiful interior. Visitors can attend services or take a guided tour to learn about the abbey's history.

The Royal Crescent: The Royal Crescent is a crescent-shaped terrace of Georgian townhouses that is considered one of Bath's architectural gems. It is a prime example of Georgian architecture and offers stunning views of the city. Some of the houses are privately owned, while others are open to the public as museums or accommodations.

Pulteney Bridge: Pulteney Bridge is an elegant bridge that spans the River Avon. It is lined with shops and is one of only a few bridges in the world with shops on both sides. The bridge provides picturesque views of the river and the surrounding area.

Thermae Bath Spa: Bath is famous for its thermal waters, and visitors can experience them firsthand at the Thermae Bath Spa. It is a modern spa complex that offers a range of spa treatments, as well as access to the rooftop pool, where visitors can relax and enjoy the panoramic views of the city.

Jane Austen Centre: Bath has a strong connection to the famous English novelist Jane Austen, and the Jane Austen Centre is dedicated to her life and works. Visitors can learn about Austen's time in Bath, explore exhibits, and even dress up in Regency-era costumes.

382

Museums and Art Galleries: Bath has several museums and art galleries worth visiting, including the Victoria Art Gallery, the Fashion Museum, and the Museum of Bath Architecture. These institutions showcase a range of art, historical artifacts, and exhibitions that reflect Bath's cultural heritage.

Bath is a UNESCO World Heritage site and offers a blend of history, culture, and natural beauty. From its Roman origins to its elegant Georgian architecture, the city provides a captivating experience for visitors. Exploring its historic attractions, relaxing in the thermal waters, and immersing oneself in its vibrant arts scene are just a few of the many things to enjoy in Bath.

WARWICK CASTLE

Warwick Castle is a medieval fortress located in Warwick, Warwickshire, England. It is one of the most well-preserved and impressive castles in the country, known for its rich history, stunning architecture, and immersive visitor experiences.

History: Warwick Castle has a history dating back over 1,000 years. It was originally built by William the Conqueror in 1068 and has since been owned by various noble families throughout the centuries. It played a significant role in the defense of the region during the medieval period.

Architecture and Interiors: The castle showcases a mix of architectural styles, including Norman, Gothic, and Tudor. Visitors can explore the castle's towers, battlements, and state rooms, which are adorned with period furnishings, artwork, and medieval artifacts. The Great Hall, State Rooms,

and the Chapel are particularly
noteworthy.

Knight's Village: Warwick Castle offers
accommodations in the Knight's
Village, located on the castle grounds.
Visitors can stay in medieval-themed
lodges or glamping tents and enjoy a
unique overnight experience close to
the castle.

Medieval Warfare: The castle provides
interactive and educational experiences
related to medieval warfare. Visitors
can witness live demonstrations of
archery, jousting, and other medieval
combat techniques. The Trebuchet,
one of the world's largest siege
engines, is also a highlight, as it
launches projectiles across the castle
grounds.

Horrible Histories Maze: The Horrible Histories Maze is a family-friendly attraction within the castle grounds. It takes visitors on a journey through various periods of history, with interactive challenges and fun facts based on the popular children's book series.

Gardens and Grounds: Warwick Castle is set in picturesque grounds with beautifully landscaped gardens. Visitors can explore the Peacock Garden, the Victorian Rose Garden, and take leisurely walks along the River Avon.

Events and Entertainment: Throughout the year, Warwick Castle hosts a variety of events and special exhibitions. These include seasonal events such as jousting tournaments, falconry displays, and ghost tours, as well as themed events for Halloween and Christmas.

Warwick Castle offers a captivating blend of history, architecture, and entertainment. Whether exploring the castle's interiors, witnessing medieval demonstrations, or enjoying the castle's grounds, visitors can immerse themselves in the medieval atmosphere and learn about the castle's fascinating past.

WINDSOR CASTLE

Windsor Castle is a royal residence and fortress located in Windsor, Berkshire, England. It is the oldest and largest inhabited castle in the world and has been a royal residence for over 900 years.

History: Windsor Castle was originally built by William the Conqueror in the 11th century and has since been expanded and modified by successive monarchs. It has served as a residence

389

for the British royal family, a fortress, and a symbol of royal power throughout its history.

State Apartments: The castle's State Apartments are a series of lavish rooms used for official ceremonies and entertaining guests. They are adorned with exquisite artwork, fine furniture, and valuable treasures. Visitors can explore these opulent rooms, including the grand Waterloo Chamber and the magnificent St. George's Hall.

St. George's Chapel: St. George's Chapel is a magnificent Gothic-style chapel located within the grounds of Windsor Castle. It is the resting place of several monarchs, including King Henry VIII and Queen Victoria. The chapel is renowned for its stunning architecture, intricate woodwork, and beautiful stained glass windows.

Changing of the Guard: Similar to the Changing of the Guard ceremony at Buckingham Palace, Windsor Castle also hosts a Changing of the Guard ceremony. It is a colorful and ceremonial event that takes place within the castle precincts. Visitors can witness the guards' march accompanied by a band and experience the pomp and pageantry.

Queen Mary's Dolls' House: Windsor Castle is home to Queen Mary's Dolls' House, a remarkable miniature house built in the early 20th century. It was designed by famous architect Sir Edwin Lutyens and contains exquisite miniature furnishings, artwork, and functioning utilities. The dolls' house provides a unique glimpse into royal life during that era.

The Long Walk: The Long Walk is a scenic tree-lined avenue that stretches from Windsor Castle to the Copper Horse statue on Snow Hill. It is a popular walking route offering stunning views of the castle and the surrounding parkland.

Windsor Great Park: The castle is surrounded by the expansive Windsor Great Park, a beautiful landscape of gardens, lakes, and woodlands. Visitors can enjoy leisurely walks, picnic areas, and even spot deer in the park.

Windsor Castle is an iconic symbol of British monarchy and history. Visitors have the opportunity to explore its grand interiors, witness historic ceremonies, admire the architectural marvels, and soak in the regal atmosphere. It is advisable to check the castle's website for opening times, ticket information, and any special events happening during your visit.

THE COTSWOLDS

The Cotswolds is an area of outstanding natural beauty in England, known for its picturesque villages, rolling hills, and limestone cottages. There are numerous charming villages scattered throughout the Cotswolds, each offering a quintessentially English experience.

Bourton-on-the-Water: Often referred to as the "Venice of the Cotswolds," Bourton-on-the-Water is famous for its low bridges that span the River Windrush. Visitors can stroll along the riverbanks, explore the village's quaint shops and tearooms, and visit attractions like the Model Village and the Cotswold Motoring Museum.

Broadway: Broadway is a delightful village with a wide main street lined with honey-colored stone buildings. It offers a range of boutique shops, art galleries, and antique stores. Broadway Tower, a historic folly located nearby, provides panoramic views of the surrounding countryside.

Stow-on-the-Wold: Stow-on-the-Wold is a historic market town known for its market square and medieval buildings. Visitors can explore the town's independent shops, traditional pubs, and ancient alleyways. The Stow-on-the-Wold Market, held twice a month, is a popular event where locals and visitors gather.

Bibury: Bibury is often considered one of the most beautiful villages in the

Cotswolds. Its most famous attraction is Arlington Row, a row of 14th-century weavers' cottages that now serve as a popular subject for photographers and artists. The village is also home to the picturesque Bibury Trout Farm.

Castle Combe: Castle Combe is a postcard-perfect village with traditional stone cottages, a medieval market cross, and a charming village green. It has been featured in several films and TV shows due to its timeless beauty. Visitors can take leisurely walks, enjoy the peaceful atmosphere, and visit the historic St. Andrew's Church.

Burford: Burford is a vibrant market town with a rich history. The town center features a mix of medieval, Tudor, and Georgian buildings. Visitors can explore the antique shops, art galleries, and the magnificent Church of St. John the Baptist. The Cotswold Wildlife Park, located nearby, is also worth a visit.

These are just a few examples of the many picturesque villages scattered throughout the Cotswolds. Each village has its own unique charm, with stone cottages, flower-filled gardens, and a sense of tranquility. Exploring the Cotswolds villages offers an opportunity to experience the idyllic English countryside and immerse yourself in the region's timeless beauty.

BLENHEIM PALACE AND WOODSTOCK

Blenheim Palace is a grand country house located near the town of Woodstock in Oxfordshire, England. It is one of the largest and most magnificent palaces in the country and holds significant historical and cultural

398

importance. Woodstock, situated just a short distance from Blenheim Palace, is a charming market town with its own unique attractions.

Blenheim Palace: Blenheim Palace was built in the 18th century as a gift to John Churchill, the 1st Duke of Marlborough, in recognition of his military victories. It is a UNESCO World Heritage site and is renowned for its stunning Baroque architecture, extensive gardens, and rich history. Some highlights of Blenheim Palace include:

Architecture: The palace was designed by architect Sir John Vanbrugh and features a grand central courtyard, impressive state rooms, and opulent interiors. The Great Hall, the Long

Library, and the Marlborough Room are particularly notable for their architectural splendor.

Gardens and Parkland: Blenheim Palace is set within vast landscaped gardens and parkland, designed by renowned landscape architect Capability Brown. Visitors can explore the Formal Gardens, the Water Terraces, and the Secret Garden. The parkland offers tranquil walking trails, a lake, and beautiful vistas.

Churchill Exhibition: Blenheim Palace is also closely associated with Sir Winston Churchill, the British Prime Minister during World War II, who was born at the palace. The Churchill Exhibition showcases his life and legacy, providing insights into his political career, leadership during the war, and personal life.

Woodstock: Woodstock is a picturesque market town located just outside the gates of Blenheim Palace. It has a rich heritage and offers a range of attractions and amenities. Some highlights of Woodstock include:

Town Center: Woodstock's town center features charming streets lined with historic buildings, independent shops, galleries, and traditional pubs. There are also several antique shops and boutiques, making it a great place for shopping and browsing.

St. Mary Magdalene Church: St. Mary Magdalene Church is an ancient parish church located in Woodstock. It dates back to the 12th century and showcases beautiful stained glass windows and intricate stonework.

Museum of Oxfordshire: The Museum of Oxfordshire is located in Woodstock's town center and offers insights into the local history and heritage of the region. It houses a collection of artifacts, displays, and exhibitions that tell the story of Oxfordshire.

Events and Festivals: Woodstock hosts various events and festivals throughout the year, including the Woodstock Literary Festival, Woodstock Carnival, and Christmas lights celebrations. These events add to the vibrant atmosphere of the town.

Visiting Blenheim Palace and Woodstock allows you to experience both grandeur and charm. You can explore the architectural marvels of Blenheim Palace, wander through its gardens, and delve into history at the Churchill Exhibition. In Woodstock, you can enjoy the quaint streets, visit historic sites, and soak in the town's character. Both destinations offer a fascinating glimpse into England's past and present.

PRACTICAL INFORMATION

LOCAL CUSTOMS AND ETIQUETTE

Oxfordshire, like many regions in England, has its own set of local customs and etiquette. General customs and etiquette practices that you may encounter in Oxfordshire:

1. *Politeness: Politeness is highly valued in Oxfordshire, as it is throughout England. Saying "please" and "thank you" is customary in most situations, whether you're interacting with locals, service staff, or fellow visitors.*

2. Queuing: British people are known for their love of queuing. If you're in a public place or waiting in line, be sure to join the back of the queue and wait your turn patiently. Cutting in line is generally considered impolite.

3. Punctuality: Being on time is important in Oxfordshire, as it is in much of England. If you have an appointment or are meeting someone, it's best to be punctual or even a few minutes early.

4. Greetings: When meeting someone for the first time, a firm handshake and a polite greeting

405

*are appropriate. In more
informal settings, a simple
"hello" or "hi" is often sufficient.*

5. *Personal Space: English people
   value their personal space. It's
   important to maintain an
   appropriate distance when
   interacting with others, especially
   with strangers. Avoid standing
   too close or touching people
   unless it is necessary or you
   have a close relationship with
   them.*

6. *Table Manners: When dining in
   Oxfordshire, it's polite to wait
   until everyone is served before
   starting to eat. Keep your elbows
   off the table, and remember to*

say "please" and "thank you" to the waitstaff. It's also customary to hold the fork in your left hand and the knife in your right hand while cutting food.

7. *Tipping: Tipping is common in Oxfordshire, but it is not obligatory. In restaurants, it's customary to leave a tip of around 10-15% of the total bill if you received good service. In bars and pubs, it's common to round up the bill or leave a small tip for the staff.*

8. *Respect for Heritage Sites: Oxfordshire is home to many historic sites and landmarks. When visiting these places, it's*

*important to respect the rules
and regulations, such as not
touching artifacts, following
designated paths, and refraining
from littering.*

Remember that these customs and
etiquette practices may vary among
individuals and situations. When in
doubt, it's always a good idea to
observe and follow the lead of the
locals around you.

SAFETY TIPS

Certainly! Safety tips specific to Oxfordshire:

1. *Stay informed: Keep yourself updated on local news and any potential safety advisories or warnings specific to Oxfordshire. This information can be obtained from local authorities, news outlets, or official websites.*

2. *Use reliable transportation: When using public transportation or taxis, choose licensed and reputable providers. If you're driving, familiarize yourself with local traffic laws and be cautious on the roads.*

409

3. *Be cautious in crowded areas: Popular tourist attractions, events, or crowded areas may be targets for pickpockets or petty theft. Keep an eye on your belongings, secure your bags, and be aware of your surroundings.*

4. *Follow outdoor safety guidelines: If you're exploring the countryside or participating in outdoor activities, such as hiking or cycling, follow safety guidelines and be prepared. Carry necessary supplies, dress appropriately, and inform someone about your plans and expected return time.*

410

5. *Respect water safety: If you're near rivers, lakes, or other bodies of water, be cautious and follow water safety guidelines. If you're not a strong swimmer, avoid entering deep water without proper supervision or safety equipment.*

6. *Stay on marked paths: Oxfordshire has beautiful rural areas and countryside. When hiking or walking, stick to marked paths and trails to avoid trespassing on private property or encountering unsafe areas.*

7. *Emergency services: Make a note of emergency contact numbers specific to Oxfordshire, including local police, fire, and medical services. In case of an emergency, dial the appropriate emergency number and provide clear information about your location.*

8. *Drink responsibly: If you choose to consume alcohol, do so responsibly. Excessive drinking can impair judgment and make you more vulnerable to accidents or unsafe situations.*

Remember that these are general guidelines, and it's always a good idea to use common sense, be aware of

your surroundings, and follow any
specific safety instructions provided by
local authorities or establishments.

HEALTH AND MEDICAL SERVICES

In Oxfordshire, you can find a range of health and medical services to cater to your needs. Key points regarding health and medical services in the region:

1. *National Health Service (NHS): The NHS is the publicly funded healthcare system in the United Kingdom, including Oxfordshire. It provides a wide range of medical services, including general practitioners (GPs), hospitals, specialists, and emergency care.*

2. *General Practitioners (GPs): GPs serve as the primary point of contact for non-emergency healthcare needs. They provide general medical care, routine check-ups, diagnosis, and referrals to specialists when necessary. To access GP services, you'll need to register with a local practice. You can find a list of GP practices in Oxfordshire through the NHS website or by contacting NHS 111.*

3. *Hospitals: Oxfordshire has several hospitals that provide a range of medical services, including emergency care, surgeries, specialist consultations, and inpatient care.*

The main hospitals in the region include the John Radcliffe Hospital, Churchill Hospital, and Horton General Hospital.

4. *Walk-in Centres and Urgent Care: If you have a minor illness or injury that requires immediate attention but is not life-threatening, you can visit a walk-in center or an urgent care facility. These facilities provide treatment for minor ailments, such as minor cuts, sprains, infections, or common illnesses. The Oxford Urgent Care Centre is an example of such a facility.*

5. *Pharmacies: Pharmacies, also known as chemists, are widely*

available in Oxfordshire. They provide over-the-counter medications, health advice, and prescription services. Pharmacists can offer guidance on minor health concerns and provide medication for common ailments.

6. Emergency Services: In case of a medical emergency, dial 999 for an ambulance or go to the nearest Accident and Emergency (A&E) department. The John Radcliffe Hospital in Oxford has a major A&E department.

7. Mental Health Services: Oxfordshire also offers mental health services, including

417

counseling, therapy, and support for individuals experiencing mental health challenges. The Oxford Health NHS Foundation Trust provides mental health services in the region.

It's worth noting that healthcare services can evolve and change over time, so it's advisable to check with the local NHS services or contact NHS 111 for the most up-to-date information on health and medical services in Oxfordshire.

MONEY AND CURRENCY EXCHANGE

418

In Oxfordshire, as well as in the rest of the United Kingdom, the official currency is the British Pound Sterling (£). Key points regarding money and currency exchange in the region:

1. *Currency Exchange: If you are visiting Oxfordshire from a foreign country, you can exchange your currency for British Pounds at various locations, such as banks, currency exchange offices, and some post offices. These places typically offer competitive exchange rates, but it's a good idea to compare rates and fees before making an exchange.*

2. *ATMs: Automated Teller Machines (ATMs) are widely*

419

available throughout Oxfordshire. You can use your international debit or credit card to withdraw cash in British Pounds from ATMs. However, keep in mind that your card provider may charge fees for international withdrawals, so it's advisable to check with your bank before traveling.

3. *Credit and Debit Cards: Credit and debit cards are widely accepted in Oxfordshire, including most shops, restaurants, hotels, and tourist attractions. Visa and Mastercard are commonly accepted, while American Express and Discover may have more limited acceptance. Contactless payment*

methods, such as Apple Pay and Google Pay, are also widely used.

4. Currency denominations: British banknotes come in denominations of £5, £10, £20, and £50. Coins are available in £2, £1, 50p, 20p, 10p, 5p, 2p, and 1p denominations.

5. Tipping: Tipping is customary in Oxfordshire, but it is not obligatory. In restaurants and bars, it is common to leave a tip of around 10-15% of the total bill if you received good service. Some establishments may add a service charge to the bill, so check before tipping.

6. *Payment Security: When using your credit or debit card, it's advisable to be cautious and protect your personal information. Keep an eye on your card during transactions and be mindful of potential card skimming devices. It's also a good practice to monitor your card statements for any unauthorized charges.*

7. *Foreign Exchange Assistance: If you have any specific questions or need assistance with currency exchange, it's recommended to visit a local bank or contact your embassy or consulate for guidance.*

Remember to notify your bank or card provider about your travel plans to avoid any potential issues with card usage while you're in Oxfordshire.

USEFUL PHRASES

Useful phrases that can come in handy during your time in Oxfordshire:

1. *"Good morning/afternoon/evening" – A polite and friendly way to greet people at different times of the day.*

2. *"Excuse me, can you help me?" –
   Useful for seeking assistance or
   directions from locals.*

3. *"Could you please recommend a
   good restaurant around here?" –
   When seeking dining
   recommendations from locals.*

4. *"How do I get to [destination]
   from here?" – Useful for asking
   for directions to specific
   locations.*

5. *"Thank you very much" – Always
   important to express gratitude in
   any situation.*

6. "Do you have any local specialties?" – A great way to inquire about regional dishes or products to try.

7. "What's the weather forecast for today/tomorrow?" – Useful for planning outdoor activities and being prepared for the weather.

8. "Where is the nearest restroom?" – Essential for finding facilities while out and about.

9. "I'm looking for a souvenir/gift shop. Can you point me in the right direction?" – Helpful for

*finding local shops to purchase
mementos or gifts.*

10.   *"Is there a bus/train that
goes to [destination]?" – Useful
for inquiring about public
transportation options to nearby
areas.*

These phrases can help you navigate
Oxfordshire with ease and engage with
the local community during your time
in the region.

EMERGENCY CONTACTS

In case of an emergency in Oxfordshire, important emergency contact numbers:

1. Emergency Services (Police, Fire, Ambulance): 999

   - This is the universal emergency number in the United Kingdom. It can be dialed for immediate assistance in situations requiring police, fire, or medical response.

2. Non-Emergency Police: 101

   - Use this number to report non-emergency incidents, seek advice, or make general inquiries to the local police.

3. NHS Non-Emergency Medical Assistance: 111

- If you require medical advice or assistance that is not life-threatening but still requires prompt attention, you can call NHS 111. Trained professionals will provide guidance and direct you to the appropriate healthcare services.

4. Non-Emergency Medical Transport: 0300 303 8389

- This number can be used to arrange non-emergency medical transport for individuals who have specific medical needs and require assistance in getting to and from medical appointments.

It's important to note that these emergency contact numbers are accurate at the time of my knowledge cutoff in September 2021. However, it's always a good idea to verify these numbers with local authorities or check for any updates that may have occurred since then.

Printed in Great Britain
by Amazon

41020667R00245